Praise for

Wind Dancing

"Deborah Schneider has lived through a nightmare that most of us can't even imagine. She opens herself up and invites us in – an act that requires great courage under even the best of circumstances. Her experience of kindness, compassion and grace in the midst of darkness is an inspiring testament to our shared humanity. Hearing of the struggles she continues to deal with on a daily basis, one can only stand back and admire her commitment to living a full and productive life."

Penny Marshall, Renowned Actress and Producer

"In her poignant and riveting personal story of healing from traumatic life experiences, *Wind Dancing: The Gift of Healing Traumatic Brain Injury*, Deborah Ellen Schneider exemplifies the process of spiritual transformation. Even at her lowest emotional and physical points, the author acknowledges love, patience, care, and perhaps above all an abiding sense of grace to see her through the darkness and into a dynamic experience of light and wholeness. In this masterfully written memoir, Deborah does not shy away from describing even the most gruesome events of her trauma, yet she always - often with humor - notices the hand of God and his angels lifting her up to higher places. Her story is a powerful testament to the possibility of finding hope and healing, even in the midst of trial and danger, and it will surely inspire all who have ever walked in the valley of despair to dream about dancing."

John Cecero, S.J., Ph.D.
Associate Professor of Psychology Fordham University

"With grace and dignity, Deb shares the public and intimate details of her struggle to reclaim her life after a serious brain injury. Her humor and direct speaking provide insight and inspiration. Her courage to go from the depths of despair to the heights of recreating her life are a beacon of hope for all who confront life after brain injury or any loss. Truly, the sky is the limit, and I'm not even sure that she can't go higher! Wow!"

Judith Avner, Esq., Executive Director
Brain Injury Association of New York State (BIANYS)

"*Wind Dancing* takes the reader on a poignant and spiritual journey through the experience of traumatic brain injury and it's aftermath. With honesty, humor and, at times, painful frankness, Ms. Schneider describes her healing, recovery and the challenges/ obstacles (both internal and external) faced along the way. Her courage, resilience and ultimate transformation are an inspiration, and a wonderful reminder of the power of the human spirit to not only survive, but triumph over trauma and adversity."

Deborah M. Benson, Ph.D., ABPP
Chief, Rehabilitation Psychology
Transitions of Long Island
North Shore-LIJ Health System

WindDancing

The Gift of Healing
Traumatic Brain Injury

Deborah Ellen Schneider

Editor: Laine Cunningham, Writer's Resource
Interior Design & Layout: WakingWorld.com

Manufactured in the United States of America

ISBN-13: 978-0-9841147-0-2
ISBN-10: 0-9841147-0-X

To God, thank You for Your unconditional love and grace.

To my incredible husband, Billy, and my amazing sons, Peter, David, James and Samuel for enabling me to dance in the breeze even on the windy days. I love you.

Many names have been changed to preserve privacy.
The author, however, is using her own name to
honor the self she sought so long to find.

Contents

Acknowledgements

With the deepest gratitude I would like to thank all who helped our family and were a part of my journey of survival, hope and renewal:

My Brothers and all members of the Christie Family, Dr. John Cecero, Maureen Cook, Laine Cunningham, Donna Devlin, Lisa Ferguson, Dr. Itzhak Haimovic, Frank Kelly, Dr. Steven Klein, Bram and Gaelyn Larrick, Celeste Lopes, Dr. Leslie Nadler, Nannie Seward, Daniel Sherman, Patty Singer, Mike Smolinsky, Joe Sullivan, The Staff of Transitions of Long Island, especially Dr. Deborah Benson, The Staff and Students at the Swedish Institute, especially Gary Lee Williams, John Wallace, Carrie Williams and Gloria Webster.

FORWARD

In the past 20 years many articles and books have been written documenting the devastating impact of psychological and physical trauma. These works have greatly improved our understanding of the complex issues faced by individuals exposed to traumatic insults and have provided important insights essential to the recovery process. In *Wind Dancing: The Gift of Healing Traumatic Brain Injury*, Deborah Schneider has added another important work to the ongoing study of trauma and its impact. However, her memoir is unique in that it gives the reader a rare opportunity to understand the effects and impact of traumatic injuries from the inside out rather than from the outside looking in.

With grace, dignity and an unbending openness and honesty, Deborah shares with the reader her ongoing journey of healing and recovery from the depths of despair, confusion, fear and pain. Throughout this journey she repeatedly demonstrates courage and a willingness to embrace her fears and to explore the demons of her past. Eventually she emerges from this painstaking process stronger and more resilient.

In sharing the many difficult challenges she faced after she sustained a traumatic brain injury, following a serious motor vehicle accident, the author's story highlights the importance of an integrative mind-body approach to healing. At each step along the way she accesses resources in all the important domains of human experience; cognitive, emotional, behavioral, social and spiritual.

As one of the health professionals fortunate enough to have worked with Deborah, I had the privilege to witness, first hand, her remarkable metamorphosis. Despite numerous setbacks and obstacles she never seemed to lose faith in herself or in the hope of a full recovery. However, quite unexpectedly, she eventually came to realize that the crisis that initially disrupted her entire life ultimately became an opportunity for tremendous personal growth.

Deborah's remarkable story should be a must read for all professionals working with trauma survivors, and, more importantly, it should serve as a message of hope and encouragement to those "victims" of trauma that a better and vital life remains possible.

Leslie Nadler, Ph.D.
Adjunct Professor of Psychology
C.W. Post College

CHAPTER ONE
The Wind of Change

O n November 7, 1995, my husband Daniel and I took our son James to buy new shoes. We stopped at a red light on Hempstead Turnpike, a busy, four-lane road in Franklin Square, New York. As our station wagon idled at the light, a large New York Phone Company truck plowed into us at fifty miles per hour.

The truck's twenty-four inch bumper crushed the entire rear of the station wagon. The force of the impact was so great we were pushed through the intersection. Had our son been sitting in the third-row seat, he would have been killed.

"Oh, my God!" someone shouted. "There's a kid in the car!"

"Get out!" Daniel yelled. "The gas tank's in the rear. The car might explode."

I managed to crawl out. I have a vague recollection of feeling the cold drizzle that misted the air. A tightness in my chest made it hurt to breathe but I gasped for air between uncontrolled sobs. I was petrified, caught in a whirlwind of vertigo so severe I couldn't even move my head, and I couldn't see my son.

My calls for him became frantic. I was sure he was trapped. As the sky spun sickeningly, I searched for God and prayed for James.

Daniel took him to a nearby car dealership to keep him away

from the chaos and the crowd. By the time he came back, the police had arrived. He tried to approach the other driver but the officers wouldn't let the men talk. They could see each other, though. The truck driver was scruffy with ruddy cheeks, and he told the police he hadn't seen us. Daniel suspected the man had been drinking.

That day changed my life forever yet most of it's a blur. I remember shivering on the curb with broken glass strewn everywhere. Although my head hurt, initially I wasn't in very much pain. James eventually joined me so I assumed everything was going to be OK. Even as my vision blurred and the world slowly began to disappear, I kept thinking, *We are going to be fine. We're all OK.* It was itself a prayer, pleas I hoped God would hear.

The ambulance arrived. As the technicians looked for glass in my hair, the touch of their hands frightened me. There were sirens, ambulances, flashing lights and a lot of people talking. I couldn't keep up with all the action and cried out. "I hit my head," I kept saying, "I hit my head."

In fact, when the seatbelt caught me, I had rebounded back into the seat with such force the headrest broke. The emergency workers pleaded with me to go to the hospital. Although I knew I was in shock, I had to make sure James was all right. A friend drove us to the pediatrician's office while Daniel wrapped up things at the accident.

By that time the pain had started. As the doctor put my son through a series of tests, the throbbing in my head was so severe I became nauseous. James carefully walked a straight line but the room was spinning too quickly for me to watch. He touched a finger to his nose and I hid my fear when I couldn't find my nose using both hands.

Nothing is wrong, I kept thinking. *James is OK and I will be, too.*

My old life had already ended.

After returning home, James and I rested together until his bedtime at 8:00 p.m. Although my body felt achy and strange, I was sure that prayers to God and a good night's sleep would make me better.

Not until James was in bed did I collapse. Pain surged through me with such intensity it was almost unbearable. My head felt like it was being beaten with a sledgehammer and my neck burned as if knives were being thrust into it. My right leg and arm were limp. I slumped over the dining room table and completely lost my ability to see, speak or ambulate.

The minute Daniel found me; he called my friend Donna Devlin, who was a nurse at a local hospital. Daniel stayed home to monitor James while Donna took me to the emergency room. The doctors rushed me through triage and ordered a CT scan of my head and neck.

Hoping to make me more comfortable, a nurse gave me a shot for pain. "You'll feel a pinch," she said as she swabbed my buttock.

Although she had warned me, I jumped when the needle went in. In the few seconds between her speaking and the injection, I had forgotten what was going to happen. The sudden pinch of the needle was a frightening surprise, and the burning as the medication entered the tissues prolonged the terror. Further offers of pain medication registered as something agonizing and dangerous, so I refused any more shots.

I had suffered a closed head injury. When my head struck the seat, my body stopped moving but my brain slammed against the inside of my skull. The concussion was accompanied by further bruising as my brain continued moving back and forth like water in a bowl that's been pushed across a table.

During all this movement, the opposite side of my brain suffered a different type of trauma. The organ moved so much that tissues across from the impact site tore, severely damaging the nerve cells there.

The entire brain is made up of billions of nerve cells. They function by sending chemical signals across the tiny gaps between them. Sudden twisting or torquing of the tissues can damage the nerve cells' ability to function properly. It's a form of whiplash specific to the brain. Both this whiplash and damage to nearby blood vessels added to my injury.

The accident had been bad enough. My refusal to seek immediate medical treatment ensured that the swelling, a natural part of the body's attempt to heal, created further problems. However, at the time, there was very little doctors could have done to alleviate inflammation in the brain. Even if I had been treated immediately, it's not clear exactly how much or little it might have helped.

Of course, the rest of my body suffered as well. The medical exam added severe whiplash and cervical and lumbar ridiculopathies (nerve disorders of the neck and low back) to the list. The vertigo also never stopped. In the hospital, I became lost in a storm of chaos, confusion and fear.

My children weren't even in my thoughts any more. I had already lost nearly all memory of the accident and didn't know why I was in the hospital. I lay frozen in bed praying in desperation to God for the agony to end.

But the pain grew. I didn't eat, drink, speak, move or even utter a cry. As my cognitive abilities deteriorated, I became more dependent and vulnerable. Within hours, I was functioning in a child-like state.

Life until then had been picture perfect…so long as you didn't peer too closely at the background. Nearly twelve years into my second marriage, I was so sure that this time I had "got it right." When we first met, Daniel and I were both financial professionals. Our careers skyrocketed as we whirled about Wall Street reaping the benefits and perks of success.

The hours were incredibly long and the pressure was tremendous yet I wanted to be a good mother. I spent most of my time on Sundays after church cooking meals for the coming week and storing them in containers that could be heated up. Daniel and I got home so late on weekdays that our two teenagers from Daniel's first marriage ate long before we walked through the door.

Often exhausted after the long commute, I sometimes took a deep breath before walking inside. Usually dishes were left in the sink from the boys' meal and I still had to fix dinner for Daniel and myself. Then I helped the boys with homework and projects. There was also all the house cleaning and laundry, the shopping and other chores.

I gave every ounce of energy I had every waking moment. Peter and David had been living with Daniel since the divorce years before, so I wasn't sure they knew what to expect from a mother. I rationalized being absent by thinking that teenagers need their parents less than smaller children. They didn't get home from school until 3:00 p.m. anyway and I was home by 7:00.

Daniel loved my companionship during the commute. He knew I had been restless during my brief stint staying home with the kids. He was thrilled to have someone in his life who loved his children so completely and whom he could encourage to excel professionally. His own career was accelerating, and he traveled with a full briefcase just like me.

The years passed, the pressures grew; I was in my early-thirties and the decision whether to have more children became difficult. If I had them, there wouldn't be any nannies or daycare. I wanted them to grow up knowing they came first in their parent's lives. Although I wished for more kids, my career would be interrupted. I wasn't sure I'd be able to survive mentally without a go-getter life to fill my time.

I decided it was worth the risk. And what a choice! Pregnancy was wonderful. James' birth allowed me to close the door on the corporate world and Samuel, our second child, was born two and a half years later. Peter and David were seventeen and fifteen when James was born and the children blended beautifully.

By then, Daniel regularly traveled to other countries for his job. The younger boys were asthmatic and required extensive treatments throughout the night while the teenagers needed rides to friends and activities. I became more involved with my children than with my husband. I slowly withdrew emotionally from Daniel, much to his confusion, and devoted my time and life to everything but the marriage.

When I was a girl, I'd dreamed that stars were the tips of magic wands angels held over the earth. They were always ready to throw miracles down to us humans. When God told the angels to wave their wands, stars shot across the heavens. Even if the miracle was meant for you, though, I always thought you had to be looking in the right direction to see it.

There was no way one would ever fall at my feet. My life had not been exemplary. I hadn't earned a place in heaven through saintly acts. No wings graced my shoulders and my days hadn't been spent in religious devotion. God's faithful servants, those who spread His word, were the people He talked to. In that hospital and during my recovery, I had no right to ask for divine assistance.

In a way, though, I figured that was God's job: to offer enlighten—ment. Angels were *supposed* to appear whenever prayers turned desperate. I wasn't sure what a miracle looked like but facing this situation alone seemed impossible. Even as I prayed, I had no real hope that I of all people would be able to reach up and catch one of those shimmering stars.

My path would be filled with pain, obstacles greater than any I'd faced before, and a bitter tangle with someone who took advantage of my head injury by sexually abusing me. In the end, God's grace would pour down from heaven in a way more profound than I ever could have imagined bringing me that sense of peace that surpasses all understanding.

CHAPTER TWO

The Storms Before

By the time of the accident, my picture-perfect existence had become tattered at the edges. One photo displayed in a frame doesn't hint at the rolls of film hidden away in some dark closet. And I had plenty of snapshots, even entire videos, stuffed into the dark corners of my mind. To keep those clips secret, my entire life had been spent molding myself to the expectations of others.

My first marriage was a perfect example. John D'Alessandro started dating me at the beginning of our junior year in college. He stood 6'1" and had brown eyes with the longest lashes behind silver-rimmed glasses. After some difficulty with pre-med courses, he changed to biochemistry. His personality was laid back, and he could focus on painstaking research hour after hour.

I briefly met John at the end of our sophomore year, and I made a point of finding out when his parents would pick him up. *If this guy is so nice,* I wondered, *what is his family like?*

I watched from the edge of the parking lot. Right away his mother hugged him tightly. She closed her eyes and tears streamed as they kissed each other's cheeks. Then his father gave him a big "hello" and…the men hugged!

I stared. It was hard enough for me to dream about my mother holding me but this was incomprehensible. My father would never hug anybody, especially not my brothers. I had never seen a father and son hug. *Why would they do that?* I wondered for the longest time afterward. *What does it mean?*

I found out the next summer when I visited his family. The minute the front door swung open, I was lost in a sea of arms. Everyone grabbed and squeezed and poured out love.

I hated being touched. It wasn't done in my family and I wasn't quite sure what I was supposed to do. I kept going round and round but there was no place to get out of the revolving door of embraces. I also couldn't figure out why they were hugging John. He'd left there only a few minutes before to pick me up at the train station.

"She's so pretty," Aunt Denise said. "John, why didn't you tell us she was so nice?"

Mrs. D'Alessandro kissed me on the cheek and said, "Welcome to our home."

The feast that followed shocked my world even more than the affection. A meal in my family began with the ringing of a cow bell hung on the porch. My brothers and I raced to the table knowing that the first to arrive would get the most. Even so the helpings were sparse, seconds didn't exist, and we all eventually worked in restaurants to supplement our food.

In the D'Alessandro home, a traditional Italian banquet began. The antipasto was a beautiful assortment of cheeses, olives, and meats. I had never seen this kind of platter and spent a lot of time trying to figure out whether this was the meal. Next came chicken soup with tortellini, lasagna followed by pork roast with potatoes and vegetables, and Italian pastries and cheesecake for dessert. Mr. D'Alessandro brought in a plate of figs from the backyard and Mrs. D'Alessandro opened a jar of preserved peaches and wine.

John helped out by secretly taking food off my plate and putting it on his. When I discovered they had a big meal on Sunday, I tried to figure out if my train would depart before noon so I could miss the second food marathon.

I didn't adapt well to dinner but I wanted desperately to fit in. Saturday morning I got up and hugged everybody. I pretended to like it; eventually I did. Over the years my speech even picked up some of their Italian-American patterns. I ate more, drank wine with dinner, became annoyingly loud on occasion, and began to enjoy the special communion in the D'Alessandro home.

My whole life, I had never developed my own personality. Instead my chameleon abilities were finely honed. I changed personalities without effort to be the person everyone liked. John married me because I fulfilled his expectations and appeared content with the relationship. But I never shared any of my innermost feelings with him. I didn't know how.

When John was offered a wonderful opportunity in New York City in 1980, we moved into the city. Since we arrived in the fall, it was too late to find a teaching job. I decided to pursue a career in human resources and found a job in a hospital. I stayed there for two years.

John could only fill the void inside me for so long. When I was unhappy with the marriage I starved myself and ran. I began to seek more challenging positions and aimed no lower than Wall Street. My job became my drug.

When I said goodbye to John in 1982, I don't think he really understood why. There was so much hollowness inside myself I couldn't function as a true partner in the marriage. The lack of worship and Christian fellowship in our relationship left me feeling even more isolated. I had lost God. By then, my father was no longer alive. I would have left John sooner but had been afraid of displeasing a dominating father.

On a warm spring morning with just a few rays of sunlight seeping through the window of our basement apartment, we sorted our belongings. As we shuffled around, the two German shepherds the landlord kept in an adjoining room clawed at the door and growled. We didn't disturb them for long. The lack of emotions John and I both exhibited was reflected by our scant belongings.

He asked if I wanted our photo album. I sat on the bed to thumb through the pictures. There we were, our entire history in twenty pages. On a page entitled *Summer vacation in Maine,* a photo showed me sitting on the beach staring at the horizon. That day I had gotten up early to run. Despite the romantic setting, I spent nearly all the days alone. I ran the entire time. I hadn't known what I was racing from or toward, and that spring day in Harlem was no different.

I handed the album back to John. Was he hurt? I don't know. We didn't talk about our feelings. We just packed. He kept offering to box up things that were mine and I kept refusing to take them. I was trying to get out with as little as possible because I didn't want to remember how badly I'd screwed up this part of my life.

When I suggested we split the silverware and dishes, John nodded. There was nothing to argue about. It was as if two roommates were saying goodbye for the summer. John hadn't fought to keep the marriage alive because he'd been unaware that it was dying.

After a final hug, he walked out. In the next room, the dogs leaped and snarled.

Soon after the split, I was hired at J. P. Morgan Bank on Wall Street. My boss, Daniel Sherman, was a Vice President in Human Resources. When I first met him in the summer of 1982, I didn't have a banking background. Before I could be eligible for promotion, I needed to become more financially sophisticated.

At first I found Daniel tough and demanding but people who worked hard in his department were promoted. He did have a sarcastic sense of humor and initially I took much of what he said personally. His comments triggered the negative self-image my dysfunctional family had created for me at a young age. I once asked him why he didn't give more compliments for a job well done.

"You're at a level where you shouldn't need so many compliments," he said. "You should be more self-sufficient and appreciate your own work."

That was not the answer I was looking for. I wanted him to nurture me more while he wanted to develop a tough banker. I made it my mission to earn his admiration. Working harder was the way he would appreciate me more so I threw myself into the job.

Despite my experience with a major medical center, corporate banking was unfamiliar territory. It was difficult to blend in with the refined senior management. I was still a small-town girl who'd ended up in New York only because of John's career. Daniel saw the potential and rewarded me with promotions. After a year I was promoted to Assistant Treasurer, a first-level officer position. By fall I was transferred and became a human resources trainer.

Although the job was a source of great pleasure, my days seemed much brighter whenever Daniel brought his two boys into the office. He was extremely attentive to Peter and David and I liked that. Every day they called when they got home from school. Daniel often stopped meetings to listen to them. Somewhere along the line, I fell in love with him.

The world of parenthood became mine as we went to soccer games, Cub Scout meetings, elementary school events and family outings. I was sure everything was going to be OK. Daniel would provide everything I needed. The courtship and engagement were very brief, almost like their own little whirlwind.

Actually, I was a storm all by myself. I never sat still. Even when we had friends over to watch a movie, I continually moved—serving beverages, making snacks, always fiddling. If I sat for a minute, my leg swung back and forth, back and forth. If I seemed for a moment to be at rest, my internal cyclone churned endlessly.

Even relaxing was a full-force attack that had a goal—exercise to stay fit, educational playtime for the kids, vacations that met Daniel's expectations for a happy life. Unrelenting standards had been ingrained in me by my parents. In addition to the perfection demanded by my mother and the strict discipline doled out by my father, I was a diligent student in high school. Whenever I achieved any goal, though, the bar at home was set higher.

After my teenaged sweetheart moved away during my junior year, I felt like I had no control over my life. So I stopped eating. On top of that, I began to run. I kept myself so involved and so physically active that there was never any time to really look in the mirror. The few times I did, I loathed what I saw.

Why didn't you get an A instead of an A-? my mother's voice blared inside my head. *Why did you run for secretary of the student council instead of president?* my father's voice demanded. *Why didn't you try out for the lead in the play instead of such a small part? Why didn't you do better? Why....*

I carried this ever-growing yardstick into adulthood and used it to measure anything I did. Despite working long hours, I volunteered for any number of church groups, charities and committees. My family ate a home-cooked meal every evening and my boys enjoyed all the advantages an attentive mother could provide.

Because I was so overextended, I could never relax. There was always something that had to be finished. If there was a moment to breathe, I filled it with another commitment. I'd stopped taking deep breaths years ago…where was the air to go?

My hyperactive nature drove Daniel crazy. He loved to take long drives along scenic routes and stop for a nice meal. He'd load the entire family into the car and off we'd go. How excruciating! I had to sit still for hours then sit some more while eating.... I hated going and eventually the boys grew tired of the trips.

Daniel was often frustrated with my inability to have "quiet time." Quiet time meant sharing intimate thoughts. I had to guard my many secrets. Keeping my distance was easy, though. Daniel was always working and I was "involved" everywhere in everything. If I had really shared with him, he would have thought I was crazy.

That fear ate at me constantly, and for good reason. My father had suffered mood swings, debilitating migraines and several nervous breakdowns. He'd even been hospitalized a few times. Since my mother had worked as a psychiatric nurse, she occasionally talked about what it was like in the institutions. She said people got shock treatments. After she described the electrodes and convulsions, I was so horrified I never heard the rest.

But by the time I was nineteen, my own mental health had begun to deteriorate. The eating disorder and frantic activities were a homegrown remedy to keep the breakdowns at bay. Fear of incarceration and shocks immobilized any effort I might have made to ask for help. I thought I was so ill that if anyone knew, they would cut out part of my brain.

If there was a slowdown in my day, I put on my sneakers and ran through the neighborhood. I added bike riding to my schedule and often rode with the boys. There was a lot of fighting between Daniel and me out of frustration. He didn't know how to connect with me because I didn't want to connect with him. He could only watch with disappointment and growing dismay.

Other issues eroded our marriage. Daniel had family out of state, and we vacationed with them every year. He wanted to relocate to be closer to his relatives when it was time to retire. I was in my late thirties and not ready to be thrown into a community for people fifty and older.

Leaving also threatened my relationship with my best friend. Gloria Webster and I had met when James and her daughter attended nursery school together. She was my anchor. When the tornado of life swept me away and insanity threatened, I would land in Gloria's arms. Her well-lit runway, God's shining light, was accessible twenty-four hours a day.

Whenever I explained to Daniel that I didn't want to leave my friend, his response was always the same: "If Gloria's husband had an opportunity for a better lifestyle, would she stay here for you?" I hung my head knowing Gloria was strong enough to go anywhere with Robert.

Emotional withdrawal ultimately led to physical withdrawal. I retreated into my bedroom alone where I spent long nights trying to remember a time of innocence and safety.

Over time, Daniel continued to look for my companionship and I looked for an escape.

CHAPTER THREE

Trapped in the Eye of the Storm

Decades of my life passed in denial. My habit of reshaping myself to please others was so effective, it became impossible for me to do anything to please myself. At this point, I hardly knew who I was. Banker, mother, wife…those labels had been created to fit me neatly into someone else's life. Only the impact of a speeding truck and the grace of God could shake me out of my old life and create a beautiful awakening.

Even that realization would take time. I remained hospitalized for several days. Since Daniel had to take care of the children, I was alone. Speaking was impossible, so I never called for help and the nursing staff left me unattended. For the first sixteen hours after I was admitted, the nurses didn't offer to help me to the bathroom even once.

Fortunately Donna took a break from her duty in another unit to check on me. When I feebly pointed to the bedpan, she rushed to bring it to me. My bladder simply couldn't hold out another minute. Despite her efforts, I ended up urinating in the bed and all over myself.

My friend changed the sheets and cleaned me up. Her every move was performed with such love and compassion that my humiliation seemed less important. "From now on," she said, "I'm going to check on you. I'll make sure you receive proper care. You just focus on getting better."

Shortly after she left, a man in black with a white collar offered me his blessing. I couldn't hear the words and his face was blurry but the sign of the cross was unmistakable. I wondered if this was my last rites. My lips quivered as I tried to form the question but the words were lost to me. My eyes begged him to tell me why he was there. When he was done, he left.

Unable to move, unable to communicate, I was locked in a place where I was completely isolated. No one could help me, and there was absolutely nothing I could do for myself. The stars, the angels and any miracles they could send might as well have been buried at the bottom of the ocean.

Once, when I was very young, I did do something that was just for me. Even then I was physically active and adored being outside. Only a horse could have made my forays better. But my parents considered that an unnecessary expense. If I wanted to ride, I had to pay for everything myself.

I worked for a neighbor harvesting corn and picking vegetables, and was thrilled to get some steady babysitting jobs. My friend, Barbara Lane, had a barn to share and plenty of fenced-in pastureland. By the time I was thirteen, I had saved enough money to lease a horse for the spring and summer.

Jack Frost was a chocolate appaloosa with white flecks all over his body. From the very first day, we were inseparable. When I approached the pasture where he grazed, he would neigh repeatedly and race to the fence. We spent entire days exploring the woods and fields, leaping logs and splashing through ponds.

Although I only had him for a short time, as an adult I was eventually able to return to horses. I took lessons and was certified as a riding instructor. It was a great outlet for all my excess energy, and the horses felt exactly as they had when I was a child…like my closest friends.

Horses had always been my escape. Before boarding Jackie, a fence rail saddled with a pillow and tied with a rope bridle had been my mount. I spent hours believing I had another life. I galloped across the Midwestern plains feeling the wind in my face and the horse's mane against my arms. I rounded up wild mustangs and led them safely away from ranchers who wanted to thin the herds. Victory was mine.

My mother lectured me constantly about the negatives of being around horses. My father, who had himself been an equestrian, figured I would eventually like boys and forget about horses. But I never did. As an adult, I enjoyed the opportunity to teach James and Samuel how to ride. I secretly hoped they would find the same joy I had with the animals.

They rode with me for about two years. A different trainer took over after that, and I wondered if they'd enjoy the time as much if their mom wasn't the one teaching them. Unfortunately both boys fell during a lesson and didn't want to ride any more.

Although my life by then was a little calmer, children and horses couldn't provide true companionship. There were no raises, bonuses, perks or meetings, and there was little social contact with adults. My self-esteem was directly tied to what others said about me. Alone, I was incapable of maintaining any sense of self-worth. Loneliness became just another evil spirit that haunted my waking hours.

On the third day of my stay at the hospital, a neurologist arrived early in the morning. He knew I was severely disabled and in pain but because I couldn't speak, no one else knew. Since my treatment was covered by no-fault insurance, a lengthy stay might not have been profitable enough for the administrators to keep me around.

The neurologist's sole mission was to discharge me. He helped me sit up, asked me a few cursory questions, and told me I could go home. He strapped a cervical collar around my neck, handed me a pail in case I needed to vomit on the way out and was gone.

My head reeled from being moved. The nausea was so overwhelming I vomited over and over. Later that day, Daniel came to get me. With the help of many aides, I was moved into a wheelchair. The tears trickling down my cheeks were the only sign that somewhere inside that body was not only life but feelings.

Once in the wheelchair, I drooped forward. My muscles simply wouldn't keep me upright and I struggled to breathe with the collar tight around my neck. My vision was blurry and the smallest sound seemed loud. My head throbbed unmercifully and every muscle in my body locked up in spasms. One aide stroked my arm but her touch just created more sensory overload.

Goose bumps peppered my arms as Daniel loaded me into the car. There must have been a frost that morning because even though it was annoyingly sunny, white puffs came out of my mouth.

"Are you cold?" Daniel asked as we pulled away.

I didn't answer because I didn't know how. Words wouldn't form and nodding would have made things worse. Daniel had to guess, so he turned the heat on high. The air blowing from the vents was like a hurricane screaming inside the car. I leaned back suddenly, moaning because the movement caused pain to shoot to the top of my head. Daniel fumbled with the switch as I started to cry.

The blowing air had triggered a storm inside my brain. I tried to lift my hand to signal for quiet but my right arm wouldn't move. Instead I placed my left hand over one ear and slumped down. Sounds flooded my mind with indecipherable noise: honking car horns became clanging bells, the voices of schoolchildren sounded like screaming sports fans, music from the radio echoed horribly and the lyrics were nothing but jabber.

Daniel had no idea what was wrong. He assumed the discharge meant I was better. No one had explained that I had a traumatic brain injury. I guess the hospital wanted to make sure he took me home; then I wouldn't be their problem anymore. He became desperate to soothe me.

"We'll be home soon," he said.

Every time I looked up, the world was covered with a dark swirling cloud. The streets, the houses, even the people took off in a twisting dance. I tried to figure out what had happened but I couldn't remember I'd just been discharged from the hospital. I knew something was terribly wrong but wasn't sure what; I knew I needed help but couldn't ask. The terror and confusion were as harsh as the pain.

When Daniel changed the radio station several times, probably trying to find some soft music, another storm started in my head. I wanted to scream. I didn't because it would have hurt to take in enough air to make any noise.

"What's the matter?" he asked. "Does anything hurt?"

Accustomed to my usual incessant chatter, he didn't understand why I was so withdrawn. Every bump or abrupt stop made me retch with pain. "Sorry," he kept saying. My short-term memory had been so completely obliterated that by the time he spoke, I had already forgotten what caused the discomfort.

The pain, the fear, the complete loss of any control or understanding…it was too much. I was reduced to a lump that could only huddle and quiver and gag. Tears dripped onto my hands and my nose ran. I tried to wipe it but I couldn't find it. My arm wavered repeatedly over my head.

"Are you trying to get your seatbelt off?" Daniel asked. "It has to stay on."

When we finally arrived home, I had to get out of the car and into the house. Considering how uncoordinated and nauseous I was, Daniel had a daunting task to perform alone. For some reason he parked in the driveway instead of the garage. Adding twenty extra feet to the journey was like asking me to climb Mount Everest.

He came around to open my door. When the warmth of the sun touched my body, I tingled all over. I had been so cold. I heard a mocking bird singing nearby and tried to focus on his different songs.

Just for a second I was back in the fields of my youth running with my dog Trixie. The breeze was like the hand of God stroking away my tears, reassuring me that He was there. That world faded when Daniel loosened the seatbelt. I couldn't see him clearly and was terrified he was going to drop me as he helped me out of the car.

"Come on," he said. "You can do it. We just have to make it inside."

Somehow he got me through the garage and up the stair at the door to the kitchen. The kids were at school so they didn't see the struggle through the garage or the flow of tears; they didn't hear my cries of pain or watch Daniel's desperate efforts to keep me from collapsing. God was with us because miraculously we made it to the bedroom.

When I lay down, my panic became claustrophobic. My head was exploding. Bombs blasted away, sending shrapnel to every nerve throughout my body. I was in a battle but who was the enemy? Incoherent, exhausted and totally disorientated, I closed my eyes. Although one battle was over, I knew the war was about to escalate.

Being under attack was a familiar thing for me. I had grown up in a strange sort of war zone, one in which my family skirmished, advanced and withdrew. One day, after my mother nonchalantly told me she and my father could never love me, a rage like none I'd ever experienced reared up inside as a result of the years of neglect and mistreatment.

I turned wildly to escape from her and crashed through the glass door in the kitchen. Glass flew everywhere. I fell down dazed but not badly hurt. My father had appeared with a look of complete hatred on his face and was clearly furious about the damage.

I scrambled up off the floor and headed for the hay field. It was early in the morning and my short nightgown offered no protection against the sharp grass. I ran without feeling the cuts, ran until my father's long legs closed the distance.

As he removed his belt, I began to cry. The strap was his only disciplinary tool. My brothers and I felt it often, and its touch was heavy no matter how minor the offense. This time, though, the beating would be severe.

As he struggled to pull the belt free, I circled back through the tall grass. There was a secret place in the house, a small hole in the wall behind the living room chair. Even though I already stood five feet six inches, I could still squeeze into the corner. It was isolated, quiet, and no one ever knew I was in there. A bag of plastic horses kept me company for hours at a time. They came alive in the dark and were my only salvation.

I raced back into the house, flew by my mother and headed around the stairs. But my father was already there. He stuck out one leg and tripped me. On this day, there would be no escape.

"Mommy, help me!" I screamed. "Please help me!"

She turned away as the belt cracked my bare skin. Pain traveled from my buttocks all the way down my thighs as he struck again and again.

I crawled up the stairs crying, confused, and hating myself. "If you weren't so bad," I mumbled, "you wouldn't get beaten. They would love you if you were good."

Like most children, I thought every harsh word and blow that came my way was my fault. But my brothers suffered the same treatment. The house was filled with fighting. My parents' constant demands and threats created so much pressure we kids often took it out on each other.

That day, as I had after numerous other punishments, I curled up in the corner and rocked. As I stared blankly at the wall, images of death rose up around me. Peace lay in those images, and I hoped that a black cloud would take my breath. I wanted to sleep forever, finally at rest in the dark, quiet confines of the grave. No matter how many times I wished for it, that endless peace never arrived.

Instead I learned to dissociate. I simply removed myself from reality, mentally flitting as my body endured whatever attack was on the agenda. Sometimes the space where I went was blank and silent, the eternal peace I imagined waiting for me in death. Other times I flew free, riding a horse over the plains with no parents or brothers to torment me.

The skill allowed me to survive childhood. I had no idea it would later allow me to survive abuse from someone who would take advantage of the childlike mental state created by the brain injury.

CHAPTER FOUR

Battened Down

My memories of the first few months after the car crash are glimpses of only a few images. Daniel spent a lot of time working on his resume searching for a job. I stayed away from the den because he stretched out on the floor and watched the news while doing paperwork. I couldn't walk very well so stepping over him to get in or out of the room was impossible.

Besides, the moving pictures and noise of the television made my head spin. Sounds from it or the radio were jumbled screeches so I often put my hands over my ears. Migraine headaches plagued me and even very dim light was intolerable. Daniel didn't really understand why those things bothered me.

As much as I struggled, though, he was overwhelmed. He had retired from his job just before the accident and planned to casually look for something less high-powered and closer to home. Suddenly he had a very ill wife, two young children and medical bills piling up. The boys were used to being taken care of by a full-time, stay-at-home mom who cooked and baked daily. Daniel had never had to think about child care or household chores.

He thought the disabilities would be temporary, just like I did. When he woke up in the morning, I'm sure he looked at me to see if I had snapped out of it. Each time I opened my eyes I hoped the same. But the road to recovery would be long and the journey made more difficult by wishing for what we could not have.

My traumatic brain injury affected my life and the lives of family and friends. One moment I was a competent, healthy woman; the next I had lost my identity. As confused as I was, those around me were equally perplexed. The accident left me withdrawn and anxious, vastly different than the chatty dervish they expected me to be. Much of my days were spent curled up in a corner.

Day and night blended together and I lost all sense of time. I processed things as my parents had trained me to: this was a punishment for a transgression so vast I could remember neither the sin nor the wrathful blow. I knew only that I was living in an eternal now of anguish and disability, an eternally present hell.

Months would turn into years before I finally understood the fullness of the miracle God was sending my way.

My kids talked to me, my husband asked me questions, but speaking was extremely difficult. Sometimes even though I knew what I wanted to say, I couldn't articulate coherently. I used the wrong words and stuttered terribly. It was exasperating for me and for the person trying to figure out what I wanted. It took so long to utter a single word I would just give up.

I had lost twenty-five pounds, couldn't eat due to severe nausea from the migraines, never left the house, and wasn't able to do kindergarten-level work with my youngest Samuel. A neuropsychologist tested me to see what areas of the brain had been affected. Even with all my issues, I thought a speech therapist a few times a week would solve my problems.

Although the doctor's window was open only a little, the sound of distant traffic was distracting. When he asked if I was experiencing depression, I shook my head. Then the hard questions started. He wanted me to match words to pictures and solve problems. Samuel would have thought it was "baby stuff" but I found the tasks impossible.

As I left, I wrote off my poor performance to just having a bad day. I was sure he was going to fix my speech and looked forward to doing better at the next appointment.

Words raced randomly inside my head. The tiniest effort to think or do anything caused a frantic collision of thoughts. Nothing I did dampened the maelstrom yet I was desperate to communicate.

At times when silence filled the house, I concentrated on one sentence. I wanted to say something to my family; I wanted to ease my children's fear. If they could just hear my voice, hear me speaking instead of sobbing or crying out in pain, they would know I would get better. I practiced one sentence over and over in my head, mouthing the words and forcing everything to stay in order.

Usually whenever the kids or Daniel came home, I isolated myself from the noise and activity by staying in my bedroom. But one day I was ready. I sat in the den waiting for James and Samuel to return from school. Andrea, a spunky college senior who visited every day to help me, waited by the door for them.

When the boys arrived, they ran through the house to find me. I smiled. In a robotic tone, I said, "Hello, I am OK."

My voice contained zero emotion and I sounded like a machine but those four words were enough. James and Samuel looked at me with relief, hugged me, and ran off to play. As I watched squirrels bury acorns in the backyard, I was even more determined to become a mother again.

A primary focus during my marriage had been on my four sons—Daniel's teens from his previous marriage and our two youngest. I clung to the idea that I would return to my old life and care for them again. I was adamant that they would never doubt their parents' love. My own family had been so uncaring, it was a wonder I knew how to nurture the boys at all.

Despite—or perhaps because of—the constant fights that had consumed my youth, I had tried repeatedly to win my parents' affection. I was sure my mother would love me if I cleaned the house, so I worked diligently to make everything perfect. That's how she liked things: perfect. A single missed spot of dust negated all my efforts. Each time I failed to meet her unrelenting standards, I worked harder.

One day I undertook a new mission: to win my father's approval. He loved trout, and the pond near our house had plenty of those. After an afternoon spent fishing, I returned home to cook dinner. A plate of crackers and cheese was arranged with sardines as a special treat. The trout was cleaned and ready for frying.

Maybe this time my father will hug me, I thought. Maybe this time he'll be satisfied.

He walked through the door appearing rather angry. His skin seemed paler than usual and he was squinting. He often looked that way when he had a migraine. He glanced at the food and said, "You only got one trout? You couldn't catch anything bigger?"

Pain speared my stomach. "Oh, I already ate," I lied. "All of this is for you."

He took over and fried his own fish. He sat in front of the TV to eat, never once speaking to me.

I headed back outside. If I couldn't make him happy, at least I could keep away from him.

Now I was trapped in exactly the opposite situation. I wanted desperately to be with my family but was separated by a wall of disability. Every time I tried to step out of the relatively calm eye, the storm of pain and vertigo swept me up again.

At the second assessment appointment, the neuropsychologist gave me four pictures to put in sequential order. I couldn't figure out where to begin. As I struggled with the task, stress made my blurry vision progressively worse. Soon I saw nothing except white paper.

The doctor then rattled off five words and asked me to repeat them in order. The difficulty of the task made the world spin. I started to cry. I was angry that he was asking me to do things that were too hard. After calming me down, he put headphones on me. He handed me a plastic hammer and said to tap every time I heard a sound.

It was easy. I tapped and tapped and smiled. Then he said he was going to add some background noise. The same sounds would play over the background track and I was to tap whenever I heard them again.

Soft background sounds came through the earpieces. Within seconds it was overwhelming. I tore off the headphones and threw them to the floor. I rocked back and forth, crying in pain and frustration. My eyes were shut and my hands were clamped over my ears. I had to block him out; I had to protect myself from his "games" and his machines.

I was prepared to be told I needed speech therapy and physical therapy. Despite the fact that I failed every test, I still denied being totally disabled. When the doctor told me I needed to be in a rehabilitation facility full-time, the word "rehabilitation" was a string of meaningless syllables. All I really understood was that something was very wrong with me and they were planning to send me away from the safety of my house.

When I was a child, most of my days had been spent roaming the woods and fields around my home. Not only could I fly free in my fantasy world, I was also far from my mother's disapproval and my father's discipline. Leaving home for college, then, should have been a time of exploration and discovery, of real freedom that would allow me to develop. Instead my body and spirit were ground in a different mill.

Halfway through my first year I met Roger Birk, a handsome upperclassman. He told me he didn't usually date freshmen but I seemed so mature, so different. Having grown up with older brothers and their dozens of friends, I was very comfortable talking to boys. I was not used to dating them.

Roger invited me to a party at his frat house. A band played so loudly I had to scream to be heard. People were drinking and dancing in the living room. As strobe lights made everyone move in slow motion, Roger grabbed my arm and pulled me down the hall.

I hoped we were heading outside where we could talk. We went through a door and suddenly we were in his room. When he shut the door it barely muffled the music. He turned off the lights and threw the deadbolt at the same time.

"You're not leaving here tonight," he said.

He grabbed something out of his dresser then swooped down on top of me. He was already taking off his shirt. I had only seen one nude man before, and he had been a model in my first-semester drawing class. My finished sketch sported a carefully placed fig leaf. Now this man I hardly knew was naked and on top of me. I was afraid and wished he would stop.

He pulled off my clothes. As he started to kiss me, I nearly choked.

"No," I said to myself. "This isn't supposed to happen."

There was no intimacy. I felt like my heart was breaking and I was splitting apart but I didn't say one word. When he was done the grip of insanity tightened around my chest. I was afraid to breathe; afraid to move.

Roger knew of my innocence, which had just been traumatically stolen from me. He rolled over and said, "You can leave whenever you want."

When he fell asleep, I returned to my dorm and spent hours in the shower trying to wash away the guilt and dirtiness. That had been the most terrifying night of my life. Even as my tears mixed with the water; I didn't make a sound.

When I returned home for the semester break, I told my mother I needed counseling. I didn't mention my involvement with Roger, because I didn't want her to throw me out for being so bad. It didn't matter, though. She didn't ask what was wrong. She matter-of-factly stated, "If you go into therapy, they will ask you a lot of questions about your parents. You don't need to be talking about that. Just get over whatever is bothering you."

Detaching further from life, from the pain and fear that filled every hour, was my only coping mechanism. That summer I began to run and swim and bike. I worked two jobs, made up incomplete grades, and trained day and night for a triathlon. When I returned to school in the fall, I worked four part-time jobs and maintained a B average. All the activity distracted me so much that I could appear to lead a normal lifestyle.

Inside, though, I was being eaten alive. Even the pleasant fantasies that had saved me before turned dark and putrid. I began to see monsters everywhere—in the faces of my fellow students and shimmering around pedestrians like an overcoat. The mummy, Count Dracula, and an evil host of Hollywood creatures leered at me from every face.

My ability to separate the horror of my reality from the horror of that freak show fractured. I wandered in a terrifying existence that had no end. Between starving myself and contracting mono, my body began to shut down. The college infirmary became my new home.

I loved the infirmary. I was safe there. Everything was clean and white: the walls were white, the sheets were crisp and white, the curtains and blankets and floors were white. The nurses wore white uniforms, and their gentle concern made them seem like angels walking the earth. All the shining whiteness eradicated my darkness. Only in the infirmary did the nightmares and monsters disappear.

All that white, I decided, must be a sign from heaven. Throughout the rest of my college years, I retreated there when I needed peace. The private rooms had individual bathrooms and meals were served by the loving nurses. Somehow the staff knew to take me under their wings. Their compassion nurtured me just enough so I could get by a little longer.

But the monsters never went away. I went through two marriages with their visages constantly threatening to rear up whenever I dared to slow down. And so I ran, whirling about enough to kick up my own little twisters, tiny storms that both sheltered and exhausted me.

As the paperwork for the rehabilitation facility slowly passed through the approval process, I searched desperately for some comfort. Just before the accident I had been trying to make things right with God. I thought I'd been such a screw-up that I didn't deserve anything better than a faltering marriage and a hollow interior. If I really focused on doing things better, I hoped He would look favorably upon me.

I sang in the choir, cooked for the homebound, babysat for friends, and took care of the elderly. Almost every day I went to church. It was my sanctuary, the place where God lived and the demons could not tread. I read the Bible for strength to face each morning and counted on the daily Mass to hold me together.

The priests constantly said, "God is here." To me that meant He was in the church. When the truck hit me, I truly felt God had abandoned me. Surely I had done something wrong again to deserve such a severe punishment. I had to get back to church and beg for His mercy.

When I sat in the pew for the first time after the accident I felt grateful. Daniel made sure we arrived early enough so that we didn't need to maneuver through a lot of people. My balance and ability to walk were so compromised that I hated crowds. They were just another opportunity to be knocked over, which could cause excruciating pain and possibly more damage.

The church's majestic interior promised that my efforts would be rewarded. Ornate stained glass representations of the Stations of the Cross filled the windows and a beautiful marble alter held the tabernacle. God was everywhere but even with the lights shining brilliantly from the arched ceilings, I was enveloped in a dark dizziness.

Two small children lit a candle at the alter. I saw tiny flickering specks and the outlines of the boys as they knelt. The recipient of their prayers was truly blessed to have the love of such innocents, yet I wondered if anyone would hear their pleas. When the boys returned to the spot next to me, sadness filled my stomach. My sons had been praying for me.

The wooden pew became uncomfortable. I couldn't find a position that supported my injured back. People were talking all around me and the rustle of church bulletins muddled their words. A toddler fussed nearby. As people streamed in, they dropped the kneelers with a bang. I grew agitated as my head darted this way and that, chasing movement and sound.

Absorbed by this confusing environment, the organist caught me off guard as he played the opening hymn. When people started to sing I heard something equivalent to screeching traffic. The acoustics made everything echo, pelting my ears over and over, and I started to cry.

By now, Daniel had become familiar with the expression that indicated I was over-stimulated. My face contorted in fear, my eyes were wide, and my jaw had dropped open. "Let's go, boys," he said. "Mom needs to get out."

"Are you OK?" James asked.

"I'll help you, Mommy," Samuel offered.

"Just keep walking," Daniel said softly as he led me down the aisle.

We had sat at the end of the pew in case we needed to make an early escape. Samuel went ahead and James took hold of my other arm. Once we were outside he asked, "What happened, Mom? Do you feel sick? Are you going to be OK? Are you ever going to be able to go to church?"

"What made you sick in there?" Samuel asked. "Are you going to throw up? Do we have to go back to church later or does this count for Mass?"

Daniel told them both to be quiet.

I was lost. I couldn't see any more. I shut my eyes to make the spinning stop and followed Daniel as if he were my guide dog. Without a sound I made it home to bed, curled up, and cursed God for scaring my children and for cheating me once again.

In college, I had retreated to the infirmary. Surely the church was a more sacred place, one that could offer me sanctuary in this time of my greatest need. Instead I had been driven out like a leper too deformed to stand before His beauty.

From that day on, I distanced myself from this supposedly all-loving God. He showed me no love or mercy. Why should I grovel at His feet for a scrap of affection? At that moment, there was no God.

A month after the accident I asked one of the priests to come to the house. I rested in the dimly lit living room propped up on pillows. Father Rick sat next to me on the sofa. Through all the stuttering, my single question took forever to get out.

"Why did God take away my bible and my church?"

He touched my arm and said, "I don't know."

I went to church so God would know how holy I was. Since He was there, I had to be too if I wanted any hope for salvation. But He had left me alone with myself, with the pain of my life, with the terrifying monsters and the memories of abuse. I hated the priest for not having an answer. I also hated God for deserting me.

If Father Rick had told me God screwed up, I would have felt a lot better. For once I wanted someone else to be bad. But no one was going to tell me something like that. And I had a long journey to walk before I realized that the accident was part of God's grace working in my life.

Before he left, the priest paused by the front door to talk with Daniel. I was afraid they thought I was crazy because I couldn't speak and because I hated God. If anyone knew I hated Father Rick, too, God would punish me again.

Hatred was an emotion I wasn't familiar with. That was the scariest feeling I ever had. What was I supposed to do with all that hate and anger? I apologized to God for being a wretch (even though God was a wretch, too) then buried any thoughts of reconciling with Him.

I entered the world of head injury ill-equipped to deal with emotion and consumed by fear.

CHAPTER FIVE
A New Life

The pain I suffered every day was pretty extensive. Stress headaches were chronic and debilitating, and frequent migraines caused nausea. The damage to my brain ensured that the pounding never ceased. The accident also caused TMJ, which added to the head and neck pain.

Other injuries multiplied the burden. Various low back and cervical displacements created severe neck, shoulder and back pain. Since the disk injuries put pressure on the sciatic nerve, the pain radiated down my right leg. Days and weeks of sitting hunched over took a different toll. The unused muscles in my back and legs shortened. Any attempt to coax them through a normal range of motion was its own kind of agony.

My body was collapsing in on itself. My neurologist, Dr. Haimovic, prescribed physical therapy three times per week. In January of 1996, about two months after the accident, I made my first visit to a private PT practice on the first floor of a medical building. There was a small waiting room, several treatment rooms and a few pieces of gym equipment. Ed Powell, the senior therapist, had his own office.

Powell was an average guy with blue eyes and thinning light-brown hair. He had a habit of rubbing his hand across his large nose, perhaps because his handlebar moustache made it itch. His front teeth were a little crooked and stood out against his ruddy skin.

Although Powell had a rather large pot belly, he didn't seem too self-conscious. One day a patient challenged him to a race on a track near the medical building. Not only did Powell accept, but he also took off his shirt...much to the dismay of his staff. They laughed as they watched the race from his office window.

The day I arrived, he took charge of me immediately. He said he would handle my therapy himself. We went into his office to review the treatment plan. After settling me into a chair, he perched on the edge of his desk. He held a snow globe close to my face so I could see it clearly.

The snowmen inside looked so peaceful. Each wore a different colored scarf and their smiles were black dots like bits of coal. Their tree-branch arms stretched out as if inviting me in for a hug. *Merry Christmas* was written across the top, which made me think it was actually Christmas day.

"This globe is like your head," he said. When Powell gave it a shake, a blizzard burst into life. The movement startled me.

"Your brain is like the flakes in there, all jumbled up," he said. "I've worked with the head-injured before so I know what it's like. You can trust me."

After receiving my first treatment, I was taken to the reception area to wait for my ride. When Powell passed through the area again, I stammered, "Whe-, whe-, when wi-, wi-, wi-, will you t-t-t-trrrreeeeat-t-t-t ma, ma, me?"

"You just finished your session," he said.

I looked down at the floor. I still didn't realize how ill I was. As soon as I completed anything, I forgot about it. I do not have a clear memory of the initial physical therapy sessions.

During my therapy, Powell seemed overly attentive. He spent a lot of time alone with me in the treatment rooms. During the massages that were standard protocol for my injuries, his touches were inappropriate. It was as if he were trying to seduce me. My sessions also always ran much longer than any other patient's.

I quickly felt uncomfortable around him. But with no memory of his actions, I kept coming back.

In February, the word rehabilitation suddenly had a meaning. I was dropped off at Transitions, a facility in Manhasset, Long Island that specialized in helping the head injured. To me it meant more danger, more noise, and an increase in my physical suffering.

Daniel drove me to the rehab center the first day, and I hated him for that. In my child-like state, he had become just another dominant male. He knew Transitions was the right place for me but there was no way I was going to trust him or anyone else. With zero short-term memory, I lived in a perpetual state of suspension. The present blew away like confetti. The future was an inconceivable concept until I could heal, and healing wasn't certain at all.

With no today or tomorrow, there was only the past. My mind continued to conjure an endless parade of monsters. The demons came after me relentlessly. Every person I met was a mummy or a vampire or a hunchback, and each time I saw Daniel I was terrified by the creatures that rose up from under his skin. Caught in this whirlwind, I was led inside the six-story brick building.

In the lobby, a security guard welcomed me warmly. It was the one comforting moment in a terrifying ordeal. There was no escape or place to hide. My legs weren't moving very well yet my mind told me to get out. *Run, run, run!* it kept screaming.

I forced myself to concentrate on the sensations of movement. With enough effort my muscles might allow me to charge out of there. But they wouldn't respond. Ambulating without assistance was impossible, and in the new environment my brain was overwhelmed. It couldn't process all of the information and send commands to my legs at the same time.

Even though Transitions was relatively quiet, I jumped at the smallest movement or sound. When smiling faces greeted me, I started to cry. My father's hospitalizations and my mother's tales of antiquated psych ward treatments were all I knew. I was afraid of being put away with strangers in a place where no one wanted me anymore.

The counselors led me away. Many weeks after that were just a blur.

There had been happy times in my life, moments when something shone through like the miraculous stars angels scattered across the velvet sky. Among all the strange and terrible memories that looped through my mind, a few joyous ones remained. They provided a sense of peace.

After becoming a riding instructor, I had volunteered at a stable in Westbury, New York, as a side walker for a therapeutic program. The children who attended had both physical and mental disabilities such as cerebral palsy, Downs syndrome or autism. People walked on either side of the horse to help the child balance while a third held the bridle. The simple activity made the children so happy it was hard not to feel good myself.

Jamie Leonard, a beautiful ten-year-old girl with Downs syndrome, came once a week. Her petite form was capped with wavy blonde hair and her blue eyes popped behind thick glasses. As soon as her mother drove onto the farm, Jamie waved her arms wildly and squeaked with joy. Her mother knew Jamie could startle the horses by shouting so the gleeful girl just peeped and squeaked with the windows rolled up until she was calm.

From the moment she arrived to the last wave goodbye, Jamie grinned. Her head bobbed as she shuffled unsteadily and sometimes she couldn't talk much but she could hug. She grabbed me every week and soon became my sunshine.

"Hello, Sunshine," I'd say. "I've been waiting all morning for you. Are you ready to ride?"

Looking up with that magic smile of hers, she said, "Yes."

Since Jamie occasionally drooled, I took the cloth her mother used for cleanups.

"Thank you so much for taking care of her," Mrs. Leonard said.

"I think Jamie is taking care of me." I smiled. "She brings such happiness to my life."

Softy, a chestnut pony with a round belly, was already waiting at the mounting block. He moved slowly and was very tolerant of different kids climbing on and off all day. After helping Jamie into the saddle, I held her leg. She threw her head back in delight as Softy began to walk. She stared off into the fields and forest as we circled the ring.

"Pretend you are out there, Sunshine," I said. "Make believe that you and Softy are riding through the fields. Feel the hay against your legs. Feel the branches brush your shoulders as he takes you into the forest. Smell the bark still wet from yesterday's rain. Let the leaves brush against you and feel the dew trickling down your arms. You are there, Sunshine, you are there."

Each week we went on these little adventures together. When the ride ended that hot summer day, Jamie glanced at the sweat beaded on her arms. She looked into my eyes through those thick lenses and said, "Dew."

How blessed I was.

In February of 1996, after only a dozen appointments, Ed Powell asked *me* to massage *him*. As shocking as his action was, more shocking was the fact that he documented the exchange in his treatment notes. He got on the table while I sat in a chair and massaged his neck.

I became scared. Being in a room with him was worse than what had happened in college. I was like a little girl, completely unable to defend myself or even remember what had happened. But something in my brain registered the danger. Powell became one of the monsters I saw whenever I was alone.

Those other images existed only in my mind, though. Ed Powell was real.

One of the therapists at Transitions told me I would soon be happy there. She said I would become comfortable with the staff and make friends with my peers. I couldn't imagine ever wanting to come to a place that was so confusing. All the rooms were close together yet I couldn't figure out how to get from one to the other. Since classes were scheduled throughout the day, a staff member escorted me everywhere so I wouldn't get lost.

The meeting rooms were the worst because they were on a different floor. That meant taking the elevator and figuring out which button to press. Even if I got the button right, I still had to know which way to turn when stepping off the elevator. Just because I was able to do it one day didn't mean I'd remember the next!

The sessions consisted of speech therapy, occupational therapy, memory classes, and cognitive therapy. Even while I was being taught how to compensate for my short-term memory loss, most of the time I forgot what happened in one class during the struggle to get to another.

Because I was so uncomfortable with other people, many of the initial sessions were one-on-one. In a private office, I sat with my back to the door and tried to do what the counselor asked. I still had this idea that I'd been bad. With good behavior, they'd let me out. *Touch the blue square,* they said. *Repeat these two words. Complete this sentence: an apple is....*

Mary Sanders was amazing. She was a petite, energetic, fun-loving occupational therapist. During those first meetings, she closed the door to cut down on distractions. Her job was to help me with the activities of daily living so I could eventually return to the world.

She helped me organize my planner, a daily calendar that replaced my faulty memory. She taught me to write down everything I needed to remember each day. After each class I had to record what happened and report it to Mary the next day. This process of repetition started re-educating the brain. Some of the damaged neurons would be repaired; the brain was also routing signals along new pathways to replace what would never heal.

No matter how hard I tried, my brain wouldn't produce the right answers and my body wouldn't make the right moves. Continuous failure built the frustration to overwhelming levels. The staff kept going, calmly asking questions over and over.

The process was painful, confusing and endlessly disappointing. My brain simply didn't want to work. Mary told me to push through the dizziness and promised things would get better.

I struggled to be good. Then I could go home. Then I could feel safe.

By this time, Daniel had started another job. I still needed rides to so many places that Mr. Wallace, a gentle and kind taxi driver, eased the burden on my friends and family by picking me up every morning in his Lincoln.

Mr. Wallace was seventy-six with dark skin, short black hair with spots of white peeking through, and a Southern drawl that made me believe his life was in slow motion. He always wore a black suit with a white shirt and tie, and his Towne and Country car was very comfortable.

"Hello, Mrs. Sherman," he would say. "It's good to see you today. How are you feeling?"

Mr. Wallace didn't seem to mind that I was too confused to answer. Yet I knew when he talked to me he really cared about my well-being. He became an important part of my journey to rehab every day.

After a while, I noticed that the same security guard was on duty whenever I arrived at Transitions. He always greeted me as warmly as he had the first day. His smile made me feel good and my mornings didn't seem so bad.

The facility had a community room where clients could go after lunch to relax. Two walls were filled with windows, and rows of plants lined the sills. A sofa, chairs, board games and a television invited us to feel at home. But even in the lounge, we always knew why we were there. A large blackboard against one wall displayed the day and date in bold letters.

Socialization was part of the therapy. I brought a headset on the very first day. My plan was to skip the meal and sit by myself listening to music. I had no appetite and I certainly didn't want to be gregarious. Talking to anyone was too embarrassing. My stuttering was so severe it sometimes made no sense at all.

The headset would keep people away and shield me from ambient noise. When it was time to eat, though, I was escorted to a table with other clients. The classes and new surroundings had already piled up my stress load. Being expected to eat with other people caused even more anxiety. The pounding in my head went from barely tolerable to severe.

I was afraid to speak. I was afraid to try to get up by myself. I was afraid of everything outside my home because I had lost all control. Being dependent on others was terrifying. All my life had been spent subjugating my needs to please everyone else: my parents, my first husband, employers and Daniel. How could I possibly please anyone as a mentally and physically disabled person? If I didn't have anything to give, I was useless.

I was even more afraid of my peers. When I looked at them, I felt disgust. I thought I didn't belong at Transitions because I wasn't that ill. *That guy's in a wheelchair,* I thought. *She can't feed herself and he can't remember his own name. I'm not like them. I'm not that broken.* I was afraid of the truth.

My brain was like a brightly colored top whirling out of control. At any moment a sound, a flash of light or a nearby movement could start a squall inside my head. If counselors heard me stutter, I thought they'd keep me locked up. Rehab was a crazy place and I wasn't crazy. Everyone else was but not me.

Then, of course, there was my lack of confidence. If I completely shut down while trying to socialize, I would be ashamed. I didn't want anyone making fun of me. If people didn't speak very slowly, I couldn't follow the conversation. Having to answer a question was particularly stressful. The words flew around my head like birds. The few I could capture had to be pushed from my stuttering lips.

There was only so much effort inside me on any given day. Since much of it was used just getting out of bed and getting dressed, interacting with my peers or the staff was exhausting. My present was continually snatched away in the mental tornadoes, and I had little concept of a future beyond getting back home.

With no God, no husband I would trust and no willingness to describe the monsters that popped out of every corner, the skill I'd learned in childhood seemed like my only rescue. I dissociated from reality as often as possible. I floated in a blank space, colorless, faceless and free of emotion. It was filled with disconnected gray shapes that didn't threaten my existence.

When I was a girl, I had captured a striped caterpillar in a jar to watch it change. It spun a chrysalis and hid there for a long time. I called my friend Dancer and waited patiently for it to emerge. Finally a beautiful orange and black Monarch butterfly climbed out and spread its wings.

I had no such illusions about my imaginary prison. I had no desire to remake myself into something new. I only wanted to get back to my old life, to find the old me. Retreating into a dark fortress seemed like the safest, least painful option.

This holding zone kept me separated from the other people at the lunch table. Between the obstacles when I did try and the total disconnect when I zoned out, it took me some time to figure out that the other clients had fears of their own.

Although Transitions had a physical therapy department, Ed Powell insisted that I continue being treated by him. He argued that since he'd already spent so much time with me, he knew best how to help me recover. My neurologist mentioned that Powell's strong personal interest in my case was a little unusual but agreed to let me continue my therapy with him.

Since there was a good possibility I would never get better, Powell used the sessions to his full advantage. His touches became more intimate by the day. I left with no memory of what he had done but with a growing fear of him and heightened assaults by those evil monsters.

CHAPTER SIX

Slippery Steps

Each day it seemed I withdrew more and more from Daniel. The demons flew at me from his form; my mind was trying to push Powell's inappropriate actions into my conscious memory; and the classes were exhausting. By the time I returned home every day, my body was a battlefield of pain. Even when I wanted to respond to Daniel's efforts to reach me, I was barely capable.

Before the accident, even as we had supported and celebrated each other's successes, the void between us had grown larger. True intimacy had never existed because I married Daniel for the wrong reasons. My first marriage had failed and I was alone. Living alone meant living with the monsters. Even a minute of free time allowed the ghosts to emerge and dance on the walls.

It was as if I were living the life of Ebenezer Scrooge. I had cheated my first husband and his loving family by hiding my secrets. The moment we'd split, the spirits of Christmas past beckoned me to hell again. Since Daniel had two boys, marrying him gave me three people to love instead of one. The task of raising two kids helped me keep Satan somewhat at bay.

But there was always the fear that my mental health would deteriorate further. Perhaps my father's paranoia had found a place to roost inside me. Sometimes I wondered if he'd seen the demons when he lay seemingly incapacitated in his bed for hours or days.

Despite all my efforts to keep my secrets, Daniel noticed my emotional breakdowns. I had always pushed him away. Sometimes at the height of his frustration he would shout, "You're crazy!"

In my mind I lunged at him like a panther. I was a ferocious beast with fangs and claws, all hisses and growls. In reality, my only defense was a mild step forward.

I was a "pretend" wife. True emotions were locked inside my overstuffed suitcase, a bin that only opened when I needed to shove more of myself inside. I was able to act any way necessary to get through the day with Daniel, my job and my friends but I dissociated more and more as the years passed.

Now, when the stakes were higher than ever before, we repeated those patterns. He advanced; I retreated. Whenever his anger got the better of him, he'd turn up the volume on the TV or radio just to get a response from me.

He was the focal point for my own anger. He'd dumped me in an institution where I constantly struggled to hide how crazy I was for fear of shock treatments and lobotomies. Anything Daniel did that was inappropriate—talking too loudly or too quickly, lying on the floor where I wanted to walk—caused my resentment to grow. The counselors knew how to deal with me; why didn't my husband?

But Daniel had his own struggle. The wife who had supported him for nearly a decade was now more difficult and needy than a child. His new job demanded his full attention yet he was in charge of four boys at home. Since the marriage had been less than fulfilling before the accident, it probably seemed like a curse afterward.

As my primary caregiver, Daniel was stretched very thin. Not only did he have to get the kids ready for school, he also had to supervise all the activities of daily living for me. Since I couldn't remember much, if he helped me into the shower after I got up, I most likely asked him ten minutes later to take a shower.

Our mutual resentments fed a terrible cycle. If he was critical in any way, it burned like a dagger in my side. If he raised his voice in frustration, I looked blankly at him, feeling nothing but contempt. Since I had been unwilling to express my feelings before the accident and was now unable, his attempts to reach me became more frantic.

Eventually I began to fear his presence. My past had me in a stranglehold. After asking my mother for help, she'd told me to "get over it." I felt strongly that if I got close to Daniel, he'd demand that I "get over" the head injury. Whenever he suggested we do things we had enjoyed in the past—go for a drive or stop at a restaurant, simply to be together—I thought he was pushing for the old me to magically reappear.

All I wanted to do was climb back into that hole in the wall and play with my plastic horses.

The realization that I was not the only head-injured person in the world struck like lightning from a clear blue sky. The counselor asked, "What holiday is coming up this week?"

I hated questions and always hoped the therapists wouldn't call on me. Most of the time my answers were wrong. If I had the right answer, it still took forever to verbalize it. This question was easy, though, and I was so excited I almost blurted it out.

I'm glad I didn't. When some of the others tried to answer, their responses disturbed me deeply.

"Valentine's Day," said one.

"Christmas," offered another.

New Year's, Hanukah, Thanksgiving…we ran through the list.

The words faded as their enthusiasm waned. My vision shut down and I put my head in my hands. I didn't know what holiday was coming up, I had lost any self-assurance, and I realized we really were all alike. Getting out of there soon would be impossible. I couldn't pretend any longer that I would wake up one morning and be normal again.

I must have done something awful. Why else would that truck have hit me? I fled to the steel-gray fortress and dragged my depression along with me. A rope holding the walls together pulled so taut the room bowed at the middle. The walls were lined with bookshelves and sometimes, in slow motion or furiously fast, books fell and knocked the air out of me.

I was so tormented by life and so consumed by desolation there was no space for anything else, not even a cleansing breath of air. Despair crippled any attempt at healing. I became a child-like prisoner in a book-filled dungeon. I visualized the windowless room so consistently that I lived there. I grew accustomed to a flat existence in the isolation chamber.

Amazingly, the counselors had been right. After only a few weeks I loved being at Transitions. The staff poured out unlimited patience and love. Marks made in my planner, even though I didn't remember making them, proved I was doing something with my time. Even the security guard in the lobby continued to greet me with such warmth that I felt good about coming in there.

And I needed all the little pushes I could get. Every morning when I woke up, I opened my eyes hoping I would be normal. For long minutes I lay in bed without moving. Once I tried to sit up, if I failed and got dizzy, that meant nothing had changed.

Daniel always stood nearby, perhaps thinking the same thing as he waited for the struggle to begin. Just moving my upper body was so labor intensive that he lifted me into a sitting position. Then he held me until the vertigo subsided enough for me to stand.

"Just go slow," he always said.

Although he meant to offer comfort, his words always irritated me. The athlete had been gone for months. How could I do anything quickly? When I was ready, he helped me to a chair where I stayed for at least twenty minutes while I adjusted to being upright. A trashcan sat nearby in case I needed to vomit. I became an expert at enduring nausea.

James and Samuel got up at 7:00. They always came in to greet me.

"Hi, Mommy." Samuel rested his head against my shoulder.

"He-, he-, he-, hello, swe-, swe-, swe-, swe-t-t-t, heart," I answered.

Samuel always came up with new ways to snuggle. He hugged me tightly, looked up with his big blue eyes and played with my hair. He took a brush from a basket next to the bed and said, "I'm going to make you look pretty."

After carefully brushing my hair, he pulled it back in a ponytail. I loved it when he did my hair this way. Even as a girl I had associated the style with equestrians, and I was nothing if not a horse person. Now, though, the simple task was utterly beyond my ability.

"Samuel," James said, "make sure you get your school clothes on before you go downstairs."

"OK." Samuel kissed my cheek and flipped the ponytail one last time before running back to his room.

"Goo-, goo-, good-d-d mor-, mor-, mor-ning," I said.

"How do you feel today?" James asked hopefully. "Do you feel better?"

He had learned it was easier to ask questions to which I could nod or shake my head.

I nodded and smiled. He came over and gave me a kiss. Although his image was unclear, I knew it pained him to see his mother sitting helplessly in the bedroom that had become a nearly permanent home. He had a compassionate heart and enough maturity to recognize the gravity of the situation.

I had gone to bed in stretch pants and was too tired that morning for a shower. When James offered to help me put on my sneakers, I dipped my head down slightly. It didn't matter if the pants were wrinkled; I needed to conserve my energy.

"I'll lift up your foot, Mom." He loosened the laces and slipped each shoe on with one hand while holding up the foot with the other. He was always careful to double knot the laces so I wouldn't trip over any loose ends.

"Do you want to come downstairs and eat with us?"

Even though I didn't want to leave the chair, I had to make believe things weren't so bad. A simple drop of my chin and weak smile made him happy.

"Samuel, are you dressed yet?" he called. "Mom wants to go downstairs."

"I'm done. I'll get Dad." Samuel ran downstairs yelling, "Dad, Dad, Mom wants to come down!"

I cringed at the sound. Sometimes I squirmed in anticipation of the noise they would make. It caused confusion in my head, the first gusts of the whirlwind that always hovered on the horizon.

When Daniel came upstairs, he asked, "What about your shower?"

I looked at him blankly and said, "No."

"What about changing your clothes first?"

I shook my head. If I did that, I wouldn't have the strength to go downstairs.

"OK, then. Let's go, James."

They lifted me up by my arms and helped me walk to the stairs. My right leg and arm were quite weak so Daniel supported that side while my left leg did all the work. The stairs always felt like slippery rocks. I envisioned the carpet coming loose, my missing a step, or Daniel loosing his grip. The last thing I wanted was to trip and hit my head again. Fear made my body go rigid and the stress made the vertigo even worse.

"Careful," Daniel said. "Only five more steps to go."

"You should sleep in the den on the pull-out sofa," James said as he walked backwards in front of me. "Then you wouldn't have to do this every day."

But the den had a TV and a stereo. The toys were in there and it was also the playroom. I couldn't communicate this under normal circumstances and I hated it when anyone talked to me while I was doing something else. It interrupted my concentration and made me more vulnerable. I shook my head in frustration. Why couldn't he understand?

At the bottom of the stairs I only needed to take a few steps to the right to reach the dining room. James pulled a chair out while Daniel positioned the backs of my knees against the seat. Since my legs weren't strong enough to lower me slowly, I plopped down.

The drop was one of the most dreaded events of the morning. As my body crashed into the seat, a tidal wave surged inside my head. My wounded brain sloshed around in the tsunami. Back and forth, up and down, side to side the world shook and turned, taking my insides with it. Another trashcan waited in the dining room for the revenge of the upset stomach.

"Where's breakfast, Daddy?" Samuel yelled from the den as he watched Mr. Rogers.

"Shut the TV off," Daniel said. "It's already 7:15. You need to eat."

James got out the cereal, milk and bowls. Samuel sat next to me and smiled with the whole of his freckled face. He was so innocent. When the boys were done they brushed their teeth and came down for a final hug.

"Wai-, wai-," I stammered, "wai-t-t-t fa, fa, fa, for me. I, I, I, I wi-, wi-, wi-l-l-l ge-, ge-, ge-t-t-t beh-, beh-, beh-ter."

"Love you, Mommy," they said as they ran out the door.

For the next hour I sat still waiting for my ride. Daniel cleaned up and disappeared into the den to watch the news. He didn't ask me to join him. He'd given up on that. I hated the noise and usually became angry at myself for being so ill and at him for wanting the TV on.

When it was time to go, he helped me get up and walk outside.

My first forays into the world were shocking. I was anxious about leaving the safety of my house, and a thick fog impaired my vision. The effort of walking through the house and out the front door was enough to drench me in sweat and my head pounded with fury at the movement.

I quivered at the thought of getting into Mr. Wallace's Lincoln. The idle of the engine was monstrous, and the open door gaped at me like the jaws of a shark. The moment I sat down, the torrent would flood my head and stomach again.

I wanted to give up. As I turned my head to look back at the house, my ponytail bobbed against my shoulders. It reminded me of all I had been before, of all I wanted to be again. Most importantly, it reminded me of my children, their hopeful eyes, and my promise to get better.

I took another step forward.

CHAPTER SEVEN
The Real World

In the lunch room at Transitions, about fifty of us congregated every day. There was a construction worker injured when part of a ceiling fell on his head, a police officer hurt in a high-speed chase, a young ballet lover hit by a bus, and a mother who'd suffered a stroke while barely into her thirties. All were innocent victims of horrible circumstances.

Derrick Walsh was already a client at Transitions when I got there. One night on the way out of a church service he'd been beaten up. The blows to his head left him with a severe brain injury. He had limited use of his extremities and was in a wheelchair. His therapy was extensive and he worked very hard because he wanted to be with his girlfriend.

I wondered how she was handling all of this. His spoke slowly like me and mixed up his words. I had a hard time understanding him at first because his speech was really slurred. What a mismatched pair we made at lunch! His warm personality and giant smile drew me back to him again and again. As I got better it became easier for us to communicate.

I loved to tease Derrick because he laughed really hard. He was always strapped into his chair to keep him from falling, and I hated seeing him tied down. I wanted him to burst free like that butterfly had from its glass prison. I never once heard him complain. His chances of a complete recovery seemed slim, yet he joked around and spoke positively about his physical therapy. He had so far to go, yet he was in a better place than me.

Arlene Wright, who came to Transitions soon after me, had different kinds of problems. She cried a lot. Head injuries can affect emotional states and her tears flowed continuously. She cried when she got frustrated, angry or stressed. She cried when she was happy or surprised. Sometimes she cried for no apparent reason. She could speak really well and found her way around the facility much more quickly than I did but she was an emotional geyser.

Arlene was an absolute enigma to me. I had no tears and hers never dried up. Her uncontrolled emotions frustrated her to no end and at times she just couldn't get it together. Then she'd shut down and simply sit there. Sometimes when her progress was especially slow she'd obsess about the futility of even trying to get better.

One day she offered to take me to a nearby curtain store. We called it a field trip. Arlene functioned much better than I did in the "real world," so I tagged along. I didn't know that, for our safety, clients weren't allowed to leave the facility without professional supervision.

We walked across the driveway and stepped into the store. As Arlene walked ahead, I panicked and remained frozen in place. It was a new environment, strangers were walking briskly around the store, and displays rose up in a whirling collage.

Although I was unable to cry out, Arlene happened to look back. She quickly limped to my side and gave me a giant hug. I melted into her arms, she cried, and somehow we managed to shuffle back across the driveway.

Neatly dressed, holding a little folder waiting for my ride every day, a total stranger would have guessed I was on my way to work. And I was. It was just a different kind of work than most people were used to.

I sank deeply into the Lincoln's back seat, allowed Mr. Wallace to fix my belt, and grabbed the armrest. Although he was a cautious driver, I was always afraid. What if someone hit us? What if we slid off the road in the rain? That anxiety, of course, was natural. The physical stresses caused by even the gentlest ride, though, were enough to wear me thin.

I hated my brain because it didn't work, but I instinctively tried to protect it. Any severe jarring could exacerbate the injury. Once I was belted in, my head nestled against the seat. Even so, the initial acceleration caused me to stiffen so much my neck went into a spasm. The muscles knotted all the way down to my shoulders and soon it was excruciating.

Every stop and start made me dizzy. Fortunately the wide streets in my neighborhood were quiet at that time of day. Old trees lined the road and as Mr. Wallace stopped at the first light on the main street, the branches swayed in a gentle wind. The seasons had changed and as the leaves danced I felt the contrast of light and shadow, warm then cool, on my face. I couldn't see the ballet but I pictured it in my mind.

I drifted off and remembered climbing trees when I was young. I was completely relaxed, thinking of the deer and painted turtles that frequented the pond near my house. Often I had sat for hours watching the day shift and the animals come and go.

My body jounced forward. The Lincoln had started through the intersection but a black convertible had run the red light. Mr. Wallace honked as the teenaged driver raced away laughing. My breath was cut short and pain rolled over me in waves and fear of a worse accident and an even more serious brain injury.

"It's OK," Mr. Wallace soothed. "I saw him coming and honked so he'd see us. Don't be afraid. I'm going to take good care of you. We aren't going to get hit by anybody."

His words faded away. My head had struck the back of the seat just hard enough to bring on a hurricane. In that sloshing, spinning storm, there wasn't any mental capacity left to process his words or register his kind intentions. The throbbing became so intense I closed my eyes to block out any more stimulation.

As the car began moving again, my hand tore at the seat. The pain moved into my ears and I beat myself over and over for being so stupid. There was no time, ever, I could let my guard down. Hadn't I learned that before the accident, even as a child?

As we approached the train tracks I desperately hoped we wouldn't have to wait for a train. Mr. Wallace knew exactly what I was thinking.

"The train is coming, Mrs. Sherman," he warned. "I couldn't make it in time today. I'm sorry."

CLANG, CLANG, CLANG, CLANG.... The crossing bars fell but the bell continued. Would it ever stop? Then the shattering whistle tore the air and the clatter of steel wheels shook the car. It was so loud I thought we were stuck on the tracks about to be hit. I couldn't see the train; I couldn't see where we were. There was only the noise, so overpowering it was like a creature shredding my flesh.

Flashbacks of the accident churned through my head. *Oh my God, there's a kid in the car!* I heard over and over. Then the crash, the panic of not knowing where James was, the cold and drizzle, my endless shivering, sirens and the splash of broken glass. My body was absolutely rigid as I tried to protect myself against something that had already happened.

I don't know how long the train took to pass. Mr. Wallace eased the car over the tracks and continued to the next red light. A pond lay beside this intersection, and the quacking of ducks brought me back to the present.

"The pond is really pretty," Mr. Wallace said. "Two swans are right here by the edge. Can you see them?"

The pain was forgotten as I looked out the window. Vague white forms floated nearby. I knew exactly what they looked like with their orange beaks and black eyes. Their necks arched as they gracefully dipped their heads under water searching for breakfast.

Mr. Wallace's compassion was as beautiful as those elegant birds. Day after day his gentle caring took me safely to Transitions. His kindness and perception truly were an instrumental part of my healing.

The encouragement of the counselors stirred my imagination. Shortly after being admitted to Transitions, I wrote a poem. Entitled *Inspired Essence,* it expressed hopes that were buried so deeply even I didn't know they existed. It started: *Delicate images of tranquility dance beside my soul.*

As indeed they did: images of being a mother again, of returning to a functional level where I could be of use. Yet *Clatter overwhelms and drums against the heart* as every sound stirred my mind into a storm as violently as a physical jolt. The last stanza drove home the poem's heart of hope: *The Being, graced, prepares to renew…/Revitalized with precious gifts to share.*

I was writing my new life. Incredibly, at a time when the past haunted my every waking moment and the present was a fragmented kaleidoscope whirling too fast to enjoy, I was creating my own future. My being, my spirit, was a soft cocoon storing away gifts of love and compassion. God's grace was filling me even as I escaped to that gray room.

The poem was written in a few minutes at lunchtime. I stuck the napkin in my pocket and didn't appreciate its complexity until much later. The scrap of paper came home and was hidden in a secret folder. More inspirational messages were added as time went on. The pieces weren't as bright as the stars but I knew they caught a little of heaven's magic sparkle.

Brain injury is difficult to deal with in part because there is such uncertainty regarding recovery. Although modern medicine is making advances in understanding how the brain works, there still isn't much they can do to help the brain heal. Whatever rebuilding and rerouting of neural networks will happen for a particular individual generally occurs in the first five years. After that, significant improvement is often limited.

Even those initial months and years of healing work best with a high level of support. The months I spent home waiting for the paperwork were entirely wasted. I didn't have any coping mechanisms in place to help deal with the deficits. Neither Daniel nor I had any previous knowledge of or experience with head injury. Life was a nightmare for us both.

Because I appeared so normal physically, I could pretend a few sessions with a speech therapist and time would solve my problems. Even Daniel was fooled by my unscarred body and got frustrated with the mixed-up person inside. One day after dealing with dinner, kids, homework, taking care of me and his own career, he wanted us to relax together.

"Sit down with me and watch TV," he suggested.

I shook my head. I wanted to say, *Don't you get it? I can't stand noise. It's the end of the day. My head is pounding, I can't even see the TV, my stomach is upset and I need quiet.*

None of those words came out. I just stood there looking fine but unable to function.

Daniel abruptly turned away and started the dishwasher. He

then went into the den, turned the TV on with the volume up high, and stretched out in front of the doorway. I wanted to shout, *Shut it off! Why do you need it so loud? Why did you turn the noisy dishwasher on with me standing here?*

But I couldn't climb over Daniel to talk to him and he wasn't interested in my needs at the moment. He wanted companionship and I couldn't provide that. The more stress he felt, the angrier his tone became. The more frustrated I felt, the less able I was to actually hear or comprehend what was being said.

It had always been that way. My entire life had been consumed by the anger and standards and demands of others. I had been taught early on that my own needs and desires were nothing. I had been groomed for this life, beaten into quiescence. Clearly I had done something else wrong and my inability to get along with my husband was further torment. I was lost with nowhere to turn.

After God inspired that poem, my attitude changed. In a few miraculous moments of lucidity I acknowledged the turmoil and believed in beauty. Rather than escape to my gray dungeon, I had chosen to stay in the present and write a poem.

I announced to the counselors in my usual stutter that one day I would write a book. Even though my level of functioning was extremely low, my plan was encouraged and praised. Time was set aside in my sessions for me to pursue this goal. Periodically I even had enough clarity to write. When God blessed me with those moments, I was filled with hope and a love for life.

As my focus turned outward, I began to understand that I had special gifts to offer. It was difficult to acknowledge my deficits, but I was confronting them with fifty other people who also hadn't asked for head trauma. Those who walked the road to wellness with me were special treasures. They were each part of God's plan. His commandment was clear: spread that message.

To accomplish that, I needed my health back. Before I could begin the journey, I needed to dismantle the gray room where depression held me prisoner. Using my imagination, I pictured the ceiling opening up to the star-filled night sky. Millions of lights shone down on me.

With tremendous effort, I dragged the first book off the shelves and threw it over the walls. Then I tossed away another book, and another. As the shelves emptied, the rope knotted around the outside of the room loosened the tiniest bit. The walls straightened a little, making more room for my new life. I took a deep breath.

If I kept working at it, my dream would come true. Maybe, just maybe, I'd be looking in the right direction when a miracle shot by. If I worked hard, if I realized I wasn't in this alone and that God's angels were all around me here on earth…maybe I would catch that shooting star.

I still have my folder of notes from rehab. As I wrote this book, I reviewed the notes for the first time in over ten years. On a scrap of paper, the phrase *reinventing life* was written next to *wind dancing*.

God planted the seed for this book a long time ago.

My new life started with a full turnaround. Rather than burying myself in frantic efforts to please others, I asked for help. My disabilities were severe and my only hope of overcoming them lay in the kindness of others. When help flooded my life like a warm tidal pool, I accepted everything graciously, knowing that this was part of my blessing.

Friends brought meals, took my kids to and from school, drove me wherever I needed to be, helped me remember doctor's visits, and slowly exposed me to public places. They watched me carefully and knew to take me home if I became overloaded. I also asked the counselors at Transitions to keep pushing me, even if I cried.

I had left my self-made prison and was spinning a cocoon. It would take time and painful efforts but I would transform myself. Then one day, I would burst free.

"We are going to go next door to the Barnes and Noble bookstore," Mary Sanders announced cheerfully as I stepped into her office. "Do you remember that I have been telling you we were going to go today?"

I vaguely remembered something about passing the place on the way to the curtain store, but because Arlene had snuck me out of the facility that one day, my thoughts connected it with her.

"Look in your planner," Mary said. "You should have it written down."

I looked at the activities listed for the day. In bold letters I had written *Barnes and Noble.*

Mary took groups of clients with her for outings all the time, and that scared me. I got too mixed up in the outside world. I couldn't imagine riding in a van with a lot of people then going into some store to shop. Going to the bookstore seemed dumb, anyway. I couldn't read unless the material was magnified, so what was the point?

I hoped Mary would let me stay in my normal routine but she said, "See, there it is. Good job writing it down. Let's go to the elevator and take a walk across the driveway."

Well, at least she'd ride the elevator down with me. She'd steer me in the right direction and push the buttons. Or so I thought.

"OK, Debbie," she said as we stepped into the hall, "which way to the elevator?"

I became flustered, as usual, because I could never remember.

"Look down the hall and find your landmarks," she suggested.

Clients were taught to use landmarks because sometimes directions like left and right were confusing. But for me, remembering landmarks was as difficult as remembering which turn to make.

With a little luck, I picked the right way. I hoped Mary didn't notice that I just guessed. My cheeks felt flushed. I put my head down and let my hair fall around my face to hide from her. My turmoil was embarrassing. We proceeded down to the elevator. Since someone else was already on board, I didn't have to remember which button to push.

Once we were outside, Mary pointed to the store. "You see," she said, "it is right across the street. I am going to help you cross."

I didn't want to be near that street. I was terrified of being hit by a car. I clung to her arm, planted my feet and said, "I don-, don-, don't-t-t wah, wah, want-t-t to-o-o g-, g-, g-, go."

My speech was deteriorating quickly. It wouldn't be long before I lost my ability to say anything.

"You can do this, Debbie. I am not going to leave you and I am going to help you get across the street."

I followed her like a puppy. I didn't have the cognitive ability to think for myself at this point and knew I had to stay with Mary. Without her I could be hit. When we got to the curb, I closed my eyes and let her lead me.

"Open your eyes," she said. "You made it across the street! Congratulations!"

I glanced up for only a moment before the vertigo became severe. Mary opened the door and walked me inside the store. "Just take a look around," she said softly. "It is quiet in here. See how far you have come."

I only saw books spinning out of control. I grabbed my stomach, closed my eyes and trembled.

"We are going back now, Debbie," she said. "I am proud of you."

Somehow we made it back to Transitions. Mary didn't make me figure out where the elevator was and I didn't have to press any buttons. She escorted me to the cafeteria because it was lunch time. She settled me at a table, got my meal and sat quietly next to me for awhile.

My head hurt and I was nauseous but before Mary left she made me open my planner and write: *I went to Barnes and Noble.*

CHAPTER EIGHT
Starlight

S uccess was the only acceptable option. Every day I pushed my mind and my muscles to relearn forgotten tasks. Although my right side was virtually immobilized, I moved the frozen muscles. Amid the charge forward came many hopeless moments. I was incapable of sitting up or rolling over in bed. I couldn't walk up or down stairs alone, and even rising out of a chair left me confused and disoriented.

I was comfortable being uncomfortable because I didn't remember existing any other way. My daily round of medications included Imitrex for migraine headaches; Neurontin for nerve pain; Vicodin ES for pain; Cyclobenzaprine, a muscle relaxer; Darvocet for TMJ; Compazine for nausea; Meclizine for vertigo; and Tylenol with codeine for pain. About $15,000 worth of pain medication went into my body that first year.

A pain-free lifestyle wasn't one of my goals, though. I focused on realistic achievements that would minimize the impact of the disabilities. So many people offered love and hope that I was determined to give back. Each night I reflected over the day, trying to remember some little contribution I'd made. Even a simple word of encouragement counted as a gift. I wanted to do something with my life that would create a feeling of success. Success meant peace.

In the business world, I'd risen to a senior management position at a relatively young age. Before my career really took off, I'd been a twenty-nine-year-old newlywed staying home with Daniel's two boys who had become like my own sons. Without a job to focus my energy, I was very unhappy. Peter and David were fourteen and eleven, and were gone most of the day at school. Being alone had never been safe for me, and I knew it.

In 1984 I became an Assistant Vice President and Personal Director at Sumitomo Bank, LTD., which was at the time the second largest bank in the world. My office was on the 96th floor of the World Trade Center with a breathtaking view. I was hired because the Japanese were so unfamiliar with American personnel policies that several lawsuits over illegal hiring practices were pending.

I was brought on board to clean up the mess. The managing director, Toko Ito, told me that the Japanese hated American women in positions of power. "You will be considered as low as an animal," he said. Although the managers needed a lot of training, they couldn't stand me. What a challenging start!

I called the employment agencies that were ready to sue and told them about my previous banking background in personnel. They got the message: There was a new sheriff in Sumitomo territory. The lawsuits were dropped.

I then met with the American employees to determine why turnover was a whopping 70 percent. Complaints were widespread: Too much overtime, no performance appraisals, no promotions, no raises, no formal disciplinary structure, crowded work spaces, work assignments written in Japanese, and the feeling that the Japanese managers viewed the American staff as lazy and useless.

The cultural barriers extended to the senior management meetings. I was the only American included in these meetings and the only female. At first the protocol was an enigma. An unofficial yet strict seating order existed and I unknowingly sat in someone else's seat.

The department heads looked strangely at me as they filed in but never told me I was being disrespectful. When Mr. Ito arrived there was a lot of bowing. I wasn't sure what I was supposed to do. I was also the only one who'd brought a notepad.

That night I bought the *Financial Times, Fortune* and *Forbes* as well as a Japanese/English dictionary so I could learn the language. At the next meeting I entered the room last and took the only vacant seat. It happened to be the one farthest from Mr. Ito. For the third meeting, I arrived first and sat at my unofficial/official spot. As the managers entered, they nodded. I never brought a notepad again and softly dropped my head as each manager passed by.

My department of one soon was staffed with five employees. I worked my way up to Vice President and then Director of Administration, and eventually I was the first female elected by the Board of Directors to the position of Deputy General Manager. Japanese and Americans alike called me the Margaret Thatcher of Sumitomo. I acclimated so well the junior Japanese men bowed to me and did not raise their heads until I did.

Although I had used my chameleon abilities to continually remold myself, all that hard work had paid off. I decided to treat rehab like my banking job. As a senior Wall Street executive, I had carried a briefcase, worn a suit, and read all the financial publications. My first four months at Transitions had been spent in stretch pants and whatever shirt was handed to me. If I made no effort to look good, I'd never be able to find the energy to feel good.

One day I opened my closet door and the metamorphosis began. I arrived at Transitions in a dress and pearls. My hair was styled and I even asked for work to finish on my own in the evening. I requested homework! That was a first, the counselors said. My son Samuel was five years old at the time and the exercises were similar to what he was learning in school. It was a far cry from those heady corporate days yet it was even more challenging and exhausting.

I continually reminded myself that success was the only acceptable option. And this time, I would define my own success.

My world had been ripped out from underneath me. I learned to associate safety with continuity and consistency. That was fine at first but I wanted to get better and I wanted my peers to get better. Then we could all escape from rehab.

I watched the people who got out. They were "smart." In sessions where groups of us played memory games, they always came in first. I thought in order to be discharged; I just needed to win games. As my determination to move ahead grew, I became equally as resolute about helping my peers.

One day I became terribly courageous and announced that we should have a dress-up day. I told my friends we looked bad. The men rarely shaved and the women didn't fix their hair. I had been dressing nicely for a few weeks and told them what a difference it made with my own self-image.

At first they didn't take me seriously. Every day I talked about how beautiful we were and how we should show off. I was ambulating with a cane and many others had wheelchairs or other assistive devices. They felt they could never really look presentable because they weren't complete.

Month after month we waited to become whole, yet wishing for that past life was a roadblock on the path to healing. We had to love the people we had become. Perhaps the easiest way to learn to love ourselves was to start openly loving one another. My career in teaching the art of loving began when I helped my friends admire their own reflections.

I picked a date for the dress-up celebration, handed out fliers, hung up signs, and constantly reminded my friends about the benefits of participating as a group. It was going to be our own private party. All our sessions that day would be devoted to sharing dreams. If we encouraged each other, the support system would be remarkable.

I cut stars from yellow construction paper and asked everyone to write one dream on their star. They would pin it to their clothes on the designated day. The Executive Director of the facility, Dr. Deborah Benson, permitted the staff to dress down that day so we wouldn't have to compete with the counselors. We appreciated Dr. Benson's compassion and her incredible ability to make us feel important.

The day dawned as a picturesque spring morning. Dew glistened in the grass and yellow daffodils along the hedgerows swayed in the breeze. I looked at myself in the mirror before leaving. My ankle-length skirt and matching sweater were beautiful. I had curled the ends of my long brown hair and even wore a little makeup.

I was 5'9" and struggling to maintain a weight of 120 pounds. I ignored the ribs showing through my sweater and focused on my face…then quickly looked away. I was still unsure who that person was. Maybe one day she would become familiar. For now, the face was filled with an uneasiness makeup couldn't disguise.

I wondered if all my talk about dressing up really meant anything. New clothes would just camouflage the wounds. Scars aren't always physical. My pain was much deeper. My first struggle with the difference between how I looked and who I was had been created by my father.

"Your bangs are too long," he would say sternly. "It's time."

How I dreaded those words. Still, when he headed toward the cellar, I followed obediently. I hated it down there. Machinery crowded the concrete floor. When he worked downstairs the equipment pounded constantly until he came up to bed. Huge bins with smelly chemicals lined the walls. When he dipped metal parts into the vats, bubbles rose up and ate away any dirt.

He waved at the brown barber chair that had helped him work his way through college. In a drawer of his workbench he kept a box with a cape, scissors and razor. I hated the razor. One day when I'd asked him too forcefully not to cut my hair short, he used it and I looked like a boy. I was careful not to resist or say too much after that.

"Just cut the bangs a little, Daddy. Just the bangs, please," I said meekly.

"Your hair is too long."

"Just a trim, Daddy, please. Just a trim."

I closed my eyes as he snipped away. There was no style to the cut. He whacked it straight across the back and straight across the bangs.

When he whipped off the cape I ran to the bathroom mirror. The bangs were ridiculously short, as usual. I pulled them down as far as I could and taped them to my forehead, hoping to stretch them out. I tried not to look at the rest of my hair, which was now well above my shoulders. Going to school the day after was always hard.

"Hey, did your dad put a bowl on your head again?" some overweight boy with glasses asked.

"Nice bangs. Think they're a little long?" one of the wealthy older girls sneered.

Most people just felt sorry for me because the cut was so ugly.

Now my hair was the way I liked it but my body was brittle and weak. Often my arms and legs had no sensation and I felt no desire to connect my mind to the rest of my body. The brain injury distorted every aspect of my life. Even though the air was perfumed with nectar that day, I had trouble taking in a deep breath.

I was a collection of random energy. I was a cloud of disjointed sparks and was always trying to figure out how to connect them. If they merged together I would actually become somebody. I didn't want to be a pretend person anymore.

I took a breath.

As I stood on the front step, I looked at the copper cane my children had covered with stars and my big ugly sneakers. Tears stung my eyes. My mind drifted toward that gray room, that steel prison.

"NO!" I yelled. I wanted to get better. I looked at my gold star. *Giver,* it said. I wanted to be a giver. I wanted a destiny beyond disability, one that would free my spirit to dance on the winds of life rather than be buffeted by the storm.

I held my cane in one hand and my planner with a tray of star-shaped cookies in the other. When Mr. Wallace arrived, I walked toward the car, toward our special day.

At Transitions, I was speechless. Everyone looked beautiful. A few of the men wore tuxedos. Stars were pinned to every chest. *To walk,* one read. *Take care of my kids,* read another. *Be a good husband; Work; Be independent.* Our pride and enthusiasm grew with every new face that walked in wearing bright, fancy clothes.

The staff helped people inside and discretely slipped into the background. This was our victory. It didn't matter what kind of braces or devices we needed, we were dressed up and we were spectacular.

As I watched the counselors celebrating on the sidelines, I thought, *you should only know what it's like to be us. We are unique because we choose to make the most out of this moment regardless of the pain, confusion, trauma and adversity. For you, life is easy. You take for granted that you can get into a car, climb stairs, tie your shoes and feed yourself. Just look at us today!*

We hugged and kissed and cried. We had become an incredible team! By supporting each other, we realized we had potentials beyond the scope of our own imaginations. We dared to be who we had become. For the first time, we had the courage to be proud!

I brought my star home that night, taped it to my bedroom

mirror and wrote another poem.

STARLIGHT

The stars exist that we may know
How high our dreams can soar.
Don't rush to travel far and wide
To look for something more.

Look deep within to find the place
Where strength and courage rest.
They wait for you to see that life
Is not an endless test.

We are here to help each other
Despite the ups and downs.
The joys of giving overcome
Any trials that abound.

The stars will keep your travels straight;
Hold your head up high.
With each heart that's been touched by you
A new light fills the sky.

The stars exist, a sign of love,
A symbol of your care.
Each one that's added in the night
You will see up there.

So reach within to share your heart;
Embrace the gifts of love.
See your reward in the eyes of those
Who forever shine above.

That day, we were all stars. That day, we all flew.

CHAPTER NINE

Growing

The next day everything was different. The mood at Transitions had changed permanently. Dress-up day was one of the greatest gifts I could have given my peers. The seemingly simple act opened the door to new attitudes. More importantly, we all began to feel hope for the future, for living full lives as the people we were right at that moment.

It's easy to become self-centered and bitter after a brain injury, especially if it's the result of someone else's actions or negligence. Our lunch-hour discussions had focused on what we believed the "real world" was like and how intimidating entering it again would be. One person's fears nurtured another's until we all stepped backwards.

Despite the encouragement our counselors offered, they were on the outside looking in. It's impossible to relate to traumatic brain injury on an emotional level without having experienced one. Self-pity led to a group consensus: *They can't really understand us; they really don't know what it's like; look how we've been victimized.* Without a strong internal drive to restart the engines, helplessness and hopelessness dragged us to a full stop.

The rust on the engines was thick enough to have taken on a life of its own. Newcomers picked up the rust like a disease, eliminating any chance at a jump-start for their own journeys. Pity and griping smothered us all. After dress-up day, more positive attitudes knocked away some of the crud.

"Arlene, thank you for helping me onto the elevator this morning," I said cheerfully.

"Did I help you?" she asked. "I don't remember."

"I remember because I wrote it in my planner. It's time to do one nice thing for someone each day," I said. "Everyone needs to do something positive for someone else."

And there I was the self-appointed leader of this new mission. I walked around the lunch room and told my peers we would start "nice stuff" immediately. After joining the tables together, I complimented my friends. I started with John. He had serious vision problems but loved to bake. He was in a cooking class where others with disabilities helped him learn.

"John, you made delicious cookies yesterday," I said. "Thank you."

Then I turned to Derrick. On dress-up day, his star had said *Walk*. "I heard you made some great progress in PT today," I said as he blushed. "You are trying so hard you *will* get out of that chair and walk one day!"

"Ye-, Yeah!" His smile was enormous.

"Let's give Derrick a hand," I said.

The cafeteria came alive with clapping. For the first time our lunchtime talks turned away from failures and toward accomplishments.

Derrick grinned sheepishly, kind of liking the attention and kind of wondering what to do about it. Arlene gave him a hug…while crying, of course. The staff also clapped but stayed respectfully in the background.

The next day was Mary's birthday. I stopped at a store and bought a large card. At a flower stand on the side of the road I picked out a dozen yellow roses. At lunch the card circulated and we helped each other sign it. Some couldn't hold pens and others couldn't see. Some forgot their names or how to spell them but everyone was finally done. I said, "Let's celebrate!"

The cooking class had made a birthday cake that morning. We were as excited as children waiting for the guest of honor to arrive. When Mary walked through the door, I yelled, "She's here!" for those who couldn't see. Together we shouted, "Surprise!"

Mary was stunned. "I can't believe this," she said. "Who thought of all this?"

"It's everyone's idea," I said. "Derrick has something for you."

Derrick sat in the corner cradling the roses. Next to him the birthday cake blazed with candles. Mary cried and blew out the candles with Derrick's help.

A new tradition of celebrating birthdays began that day. The cooking group stayed busy making goodies for each and every party. Positive encouragement became part of our everyday conversations. Everyone benefited. By helping others, I helped myself more than I had ever thought possible.

The support and love from my peers fed the place in me that had been empty my entire life. I grew strong, began to shine brilliantly, and opened my heart to the next challenge. Deep in my cocoon, I was changing. One day I would be able to fly. Until then, I waited for the calling that would inspire a new life, a dance on the wind.

Before the accident I had been riding a horse that belonged to my friend Lucy Cuenick. She encouraged me to try riding again to help strengthen my body. Getting back on a horse would certainly increase my confidence and sense of accomplishment.

The stable was located in Brookville, New York. A dirt driveway curved in from the tree-lined street to a red barn, which gave the farm its name. The Red Barn had three separate stables, a huge indoor riding ring and two outdoor rings. Horses were turned out to graze in numerous paddocks. A track bordered some of the fields and woods that were scattered throughout the property.

Lucy's horse Buttons was a bay, brown with a black mane, tail and legs. He was a quarter horse gelding and stood sixteen hands. With a rounded barrel of a belly and a wide chest, he was good-natured and stayed quite calm as I struggled on and off. Even though I sometimes jabbed my heel into his side when mounting, he always kept his ears forward and was very forgiving.

Lucy and my friend, Celeste Lopes, were both instrumental in helping me ride. I had started leasing Buttons a month before the car accident and paid Lucy to ride him three days per week. She was a rugged woman a few inches shorter than me with short wavy hair and glasses.

Although she shook my hand firmly when we first met, she had a shyness about her. Her eyes would dart down when we talked and she only seemed truly relaxed when she groomed Buttons. After a riding lesson and a few hours of sharing, we bonded as friends. She was single, worked for an insurance company, and cared for her mother who suffered from dementia. Buttons was her escape, a feeling I could relate to.

Celeste, on the other hand, was my inspiration. Standing 4'10", her black hair was always tied in a ponytail, and she had an athletic build. Even though she was blind, nothing stopped her. She loved sports and she maneuvered her horse with supreme confidence in the ring. When she wasn't enjoying her leisure time, she worked as an assistant district attorney. Knowing she had overcome obstacles inspired me to listen to her when I became disabled.

While Lucy remained more of a barn friend, Celeste was an important part of my life away from the stables. She spent a lot of time encouraging me to do the things I loved. Celeste skied, hiked, rode bikes, and loved to go to water parks and scream on the scary rides. Later when she found out I had once been an expert skier,

I resumed skiing in an adaptive program because Celeste said I could.

She often took me shopping. I would be her eyes and she would be my brain. She would remember what I went to the store for, where the car was parked, and negotiate our way through busy shopping malls. She dragged and pushed me into the world, always with complete confidence that I would succeed.

Riding seemed like a far-away notion, as unreachable as when I had been a child. Living in farm country where horses were everywhere had been one of my greatest joys. Occasionally they would escape and end up in my father's garden to feast on row after row of carrots. I wanted so badly to catch a stray horse that I kept sugar cubes on my dresser along with a rope. One day, I hoped, I would capture one of those equine visitors and go for a ride.

My big chance arrived on a frosty spring morning. My bedroom was in the back of the house and faced the vegetable garden. Everyone was asleep when a soft nicker reached my ears. I grabbed the sugar and the rope and crawled out the window onto the porch roof. After inching over to the garage, I jumped several feet to the ground.

The horses paid little attention to me. They were both bays, and the closest one looked up with interest when she noticed my outstretched hand. She neighed when she saw the sugar. As she walked over, I let the cubes fall to the ground so she would put her head down.

I slipped the rope around her neck. I wanted to scream for joy as she lifted her head and waited for me to do something. I was a tiny, seven-year-old girl with a thin rope controlling a big horse! I led her over to the porch stairs. The grass was frozen, my feet were tingling, and it was so cold that I could see my breath but I was happy. When I climbed onto the top step, I grabbed a handful of mane and jumped onto her back.

She started walking as I twisted around to sit up. Her body was warm against my cold legs. I was riding! This was my dream come true. I didn't know what to do other than hold onto the rope so we wandered back toward the pasture.

When my dog Trixie saw us walking away, she started barking. The sound startled the mare. She pranced sideways, and I bounced right off. As the horses galloped away, I grabbed the rope and headed after them.

Running through the fields was thrilling. Without more sugar, I couldn't coax the pair to stand still long enough for me to touch them. It became a game of tag with a fantastic prize: a ride on a horse! There were no anxious stomachaches, I was oblivious to the frost, and although I wore only my blue nightgown, I was warm inside and out.

I never got a second ride that day. I had to be content with the fantasy of changing into a star-filled constellation so I could ride a blazing heavenly stallion for eternity. Lucy and Celeste told me to keep thinking of those shooting stars when they brought me to the stable after the accident.

As they helped me into the saddle, I was no longer the fearless rider who had mounted an unknown horse bareback and without a bridle. My right leg was so weak that one of my friends had to swing it over the horse's back and place it in the stirrup. Two people held my legs while a third person took the reins. That high up, even with a helmet, I was shaking.

"I, I, I can-, can-, can't r-r-r-ride any-, more," I said.

We started walking.

I clung to the saddle with one hand and buried my other fist in the horse's mane. I stared at the ground hoping I wouldn't fall. It was so high! A tumble would surely cause a re-injury despite the helmet.

Then the rhythm of the horse's gait broke through the fear. It was such a soothing motion. The rocking coaxed my body to relax. The horse's legs became my own. Suddenly I could travel great distances without stumbling and struggling. I could look around and enjoy the day; I could ride!

I grabbed the reins. My side walkers stayed with me while encouraging me to take control. I cried that first time in the saddle. I had taught plenty of disabled people how to ride and remembered how delighted they had been to be free of their bodies' restrictions. That day I was as happy as Jamie, the girl with Downs syndrome.

Although I didn't think it was possible for anyone else to feel so blessed, my friends were nearly as happy. "Before the accident," they said, "you were always a giver. Now it's your turn to receive."

"One day," I stuttered, "I will ride by myself, and I will jump!"

The next time I went to the barn, I took a big yellow star with the words *Let Your Dreams Soar.* My friends took my picture while I was mounted. I proudly brought the photograph to Transitions. I was pursuing my goal and enjoying a sport that I loved. I was doing it differently than I had ever imagined, with side walkers and a leader, but I was riding!

I worked harder than ever to regain my physical strength. One day I would jump horses over fences. Some of my peers couldn't understand my enthusiasm. After all, to go from being an accomplished equestrian to receiving pony rides couldn't really be called riding.

Yet for me, it was a major step in the right direction. If I adjusted my expectations and appreciated what I could do at the moment, I would find happiness in that moment. Pleasure and pride would give me the strength to push harder. Most of all, I needed to remember what it felt like to be happy so I could work toward feeling that way again.

Change can be a good thing. I said it over and over to convince myself it was true. I'm sure my peers thought me silly because I actually wasn't very adaptable at all. I talked about change yet everyone knew I didn't like the smallest variation in my schedule at Transitions.

Take, for example, lunchtime. Every week the menu repeated itself. Every Friday was pizza day. I enjoyed it so much that at the beginning of each week I wrote *pizza* in capital letters in my planner. I wasn't able to taste the difference between many foods but the pizza was spicy enough that I could detect a slight pleasing flavor.

One Friday pizza was not served. Suddenly I stopped proclaiming the need to be flexible and had a miniature screaming fit!

My peers kept eating while I ranted and raved. We all got frustrated by different things. Because most of us had little ability to control our emotions, we generally tolerated each others' outbursts. As I moaned about the pizza, several people suggested I try the egg salad that had been served in its place.

I didn't like that idea, either. Everyone ate the egg salad and waited for me to simmer down. But I was deep into my rebellion. I had little control over anything in my life so refusing to eat allowed me to take charge. I'm not sure what I was taking charge of, though, because my stomach ached terribly from hunger all afternoon.

Years later I looked back in my planner and saw a note written at the end of the day: *Next time eat the egg salad!*

CHAPTER TEN

Miracles

Although the silk cocoon that nourished me was too small to hold anyone else, I wasn't alone. God found enough room to squeeze in there with me. As I meditated to music, He filled my body and surrounded me with peace. My mind stopped racing and the explosions diffused.

During one moment of tranquility, I pictured myself walking on the beach early in the morning. The salty air was warm against my skin and the wind gently brushed my hair. The sunrise brought a bright red glow to the horizon as little birds searched the tidal pools. They ran just ahead of the incoming surf, never tired of teasing the sea. Footprints were all that remained as they flew away.

I wanted my delicate and fragile body to do the unimaginable: to take flight, even if only in my dreams. Although I was unable to see or speak clearly and had ongoing memory problems, while reflecting I was blessed with twenty minutes of clarity. My soul opened up and this is what poured out.

WIND DANCING

A multicolored caterpillar lazily basked in the sun with its diminutive antennae sensitive to the gentle wind. On this enchanted spring day, the milkweed plant was a paradise providing abundant sustenance. The fibers of the plant seemed to tickle the underside of the caterpillar for it awkwardly arched upwards as if to play with the breeze. A thunderous snap and crash reduced the caterpillar to a twisted unrecognizable configuration at the bottom of the glass jar. Instantaneously there was only darkness and then stagnation as a milkweed branch landed overhead.

Bounced around repeatedly in this "new world," the caterpillar gave the impression of lifelessness. It remained immobile for days, until eventually it wriggled to a leaf and painstakingly designed its chrysalis. It then retreated to this dark, constricting place of safety and also of terror... for without warning the jar was jostled repeatedly, and the caterpillar's precariously placed nest was vulnerable to destruction.

And then, there was the miracle. The chrysalis' outer shell unfolded magically. The Monarch butterfly within stretched its stiff legs, opened its eyes and unfolded wings of magnificence. With trepidation the butterfly gingerly opened and closed its wings, which made Mother Nature sigh with pride. As the moisture evaporated from the delicate wings, the butterfly looked at the world for the first time with amazement and awe. Energized by the boundless beauty, the butterfly gently stretched and flapped its wings in anticipation of flight.

Soaring upward the butterfly hovered in suspended animation as it captured an aerial view of its past existence. The creation of delight descended and ascended again and again, exhilarated and enjoying an effortless dance with the wind.

After finishing my brief dance in the wind of clarity, the disabilities resumed control. I stumbled back into my world of pain and fear.

The next morning I woke up with *Wind Dancing* tucked under the covers along with Samuel. He had suffered with asthma during the night and his breathing had been labored. I soothed him as always by massaging his back and chest. As he lay in my arms breathing more easily, I felt a drive to pursue this hands-on healing work as my profession.

I looked at the scrap of paper and the scribbled words. To have been able to write that was truly a miracle. Something special had happened, and I shared the treasure at Transitions. Someone made copies and circulated it among the staff and clients. The idea of such an exhilarating dance made my peers and counselors sigh.

I proudly showed the story to Daniel that night. "I wro-, wro-, wro-t-te thi-, thi-, thi-s-s-s," I said.

He took the wrinkled paper, read for long minutes then said, "This is really beautiful. I can't believe you wrote this. It's really incredible."

He took the paper and I didn't see it for quite some time. One day as I was resting in a patch of sunlight in the den, Daniel came in. "Look what I have for you," he said.

He helped me open a box. Inside was *Wind Dancing* typeset on fancy bond. The paper had soft tones of pink with a watermark Monarch butterfly stretched out in the center. The matting was a darker shade of pink and the frame was gold.

"It's be-, be-, be-u-, t-t-t, ful," I stammered. Even though I was unable to read the words without magnification, I knew the story by heart. I saw the faint image of the butterfly and knew Daniel understood the importance of this one piece. I wanted to write more but neither of us knew if that would be possible.

He assisted me off the sofa and led me into the dining room. After settling me in a chair, he hung the picture where it stood out against the navy wallpaper in a field of pink flowers. All our visitors traveled through the dining room to the kitchen and den, so the placement was prominent. The message of hope beckoned everyone who read it.

I wanted to unleash that energy, to pursue my new purpose. My calling had been born from a butterfly's flight. My life experiences had filled me with compassion and God had blessed me with the openness to hear His plan. There was a gift in my hands, the gift of therapeutic touch.

I walked into the lunch room with a CD player, a few CDs, a little massage cream, and vivid aspirations. When I asked Arlene if she wanted a massage, her response was enthusiastic. Afterward she felt great. She was in less pain, was calmer, and wanted an appointment for another session! Once she told the rest of our team how wonderful the massage and meditation had been, my planner was filled with appointments every day.

We ate lunch quickly and disappeared into a supply closet for privacy. When I touched peoples' heads, the energy poured from my hands in a loving stream. Light surrounded us, heat poured from my palms, and God was there. My mission was clear to me and those around me.

My calling wasn't so obvious to the counselors when I was caught. My new career came to an abrupt end. Since I didn't have a license to touch, I couldn't continue massaging. Their concerns were entirely understandable. I stuttered that one day I would be a massage therapist with my own practice specializing in pain and stress relief.

I was ambulating with a cane, unsteady on my feet, constantly re-injuring myself as a result of falling and tripping, and in a physical rehabilitation program that would continue for years. I couldn't remember anything without my planner and was in chronic pain. Becoming a massage therapist meant enrolling in a complicated and lengthy academic program, which most people would have thought was beyond my abilities.

I didn't know about the training requirements. I only knew hands-on healing was part of my destiny. If the counselors thought this idea was out of my reach, their faces showed no doubts. Instead there was only admiration for the resolute manner in which I approached challenges.

My wings were starting to grow.

Everyone forgets things; everyone misplaces their keys or the folder they brought home from work. For me, though, memory deficits were beyond a brief lapse. Remembering what I was supposed to be doing was incredibly taxing.

In rehab everything was written down but at home, I often put the planner down and forget where it was. The boys routinely raced around trying to find mommy's book. Eventually constant reminders from my children trained me to put the planner in the same place.

My two older sons moved out to start their own careers while I was relearning the basic skills of life. James and Samuel, the younger boys, became tremendously sympathetic and patient. They assumed responsibilities around the house and were very protective. They filled in my words when I forgot what to say, carried things for me, helped me with everyday activities, and gave me more motivation to heal.

To show my appreciation, I tried to make cookies. No one was home so I thought it would be a grand surprise to come home to the smells and tastes that had been absent for so long. Because I had baked constantly in the past, I thought it would be easy.

Although I used a recipe, I couldn't keep track of the steps. Instead there was a lot of improvisation. If the recipe called for two cups of flour, I kept adding flour while supposedly counting. Maybe I counted to one then counted to two several times. I don't know.

After I mixed sugar into the flour, I couldn't remember what was in the bowl. White flour mixed with white sugar looked like it was all flour. After I cracked the eggs, I forgot how many I'd cracked. I finally managed to get the dough dropped onto a cookie sheet but forgot they were in the oven. Since my sense of smell had been severely compromised, I didn't notice the burnt odor permeating the house.

When I happened to walk back into the kitchen, smoke was pouring from the oven. I stood perfectly still not knowing what to do. At first I didn't recognize the danger. When I did, it took a long time for me to walk over, turn the oven off, and remove the cookies. Since I forgot the tray was hot, I burned my fingers trying to take it out without an oven mitt.

After relaying the story to Mary at Transitions, her expression changed from interest to alarm. She must have said something to my family because I wasn't allowed in the kitchen alone after that. James caught me trying to make brownies a few days later and I had a temper tantrum when he wouldn't allow me to bake.

Mary immediately put me into a special occupational therapy cooking class. There I was taught how to follow a recipe by highlighting each completed step and to use timers. Notes were placed on the timers so that when I shut them off, I knew what I was supposed to do. There was even a reminder to use a potholder!

Completing the cooking class was one thing. Setting up the kitchen to meet my needs was another. Mary actually came to my house to help me organize everything so it would be safe for me to be in there alone. She was wonderful, and the rearranged kitchen was a solid symbol of my progress.

I still needed a timer, though. Such a little thing, that timer. It was inexpensive and hardly worth a second glance. But buying one cost an entire day and every ounce of energy I could muster.

Mary took Arlene and me to Target. Even though I was nervous, I wanted to go. In order to be discharged from Transitions, I had to achieve certain goals. One of Mary's goals for me was to handle myself in crowds. I had children to take care of and I needed to be able to cope with all the stimulation that goes along with shopping.

"The van is waiting," Mary announced.

Arlene and I hugged. She cried and I smiled as we set off down the hall.

It was a sunny spring day with a freshness to the air. When I glanced up at the beautiful blue sky, I saw the brightest, fluffiest clouds ever. As a child, I used to lie in the hayfields and make up stories about different characters I saw in the cloud formations. Today I saw children rushing down to greet me.

"Look, Arlene," I said. "My kids are in those clouds. Can you see them? Can you see the children?"

Arlene didn't have quite the same imagination. She humored me by quickly scanning the sky. "I know you can't see very well," she said, "but I can assure you that your children are not up there."

She didn't get it. That was OK because it was my world.

Mary herded us toward the van. Rick Jones, a life skills trainer, joined us. He was well over six feet tall, very thin, and had dark brown hair. "Careful now," he said as he helped us. "Take your time. We aren't in any rush. It's a beautiful day so let's enjoy it together."

He helped us fastened our seatbelts and took his place in the front. I hadn't ridden anywhere with Mary driving and became nervous. I wasn't comfortable with change. I wished Mr. Wallace was sitting behind the wheel.

"I need to get some picture frames," Arlene said. "What are you getting?"

I panicked. I had forgotten why I was making this trip.

"Just look in your planner," she said.

I fumbled in my purse and opened the book. I had written *Get a timer.*

She started to cry. She knew I loved to cook and that I had lost cooking privileges at home. Her tears were from the joy of knowing Mary was working with me to achieve an important bit of independence.

"One day I'll stop this crying," she said with a laugh.

"One da-, da-, da-, day I, I, I wi-, will cr-, cr-, cry," I said.

She cried more while I smiled.

I looked out the window as the blurry world sped by. My vision had improved a little by now but when pressured I regressed. Mary parked in a handicapped spot right next to the door. I had forgotten, again, what I was there for.

"Debbie," Mary said, "why don't you look in your planner and see what you need?"

I looked again and we went inside. It was 11:00 a.m. and even though there weren't a lot of people, I automatically looked down. Mary stopped me from blocking out the world.

"Debbie, please help me," she said. "I need that big plastic bin on the top shelf and I can't reach it. You are tall. You can get it."

Without thinking, I looked up. I easily pulled down the bin and placed it in her arms.

"Help me carry it, please," she said. "It's too big for me to manage alone."

I carried one end and she carried the other. Arlene had left to shop with Rick, so Mary and I walked the store together. She asked me to help her reach other objects until we made our way to the baking aisle.

"Put the bin down for a minute and help me find your timer," she said.

Together we picked out one. By then we were done shopping and I was done mentally. At the register I began to check out from the world. Rick took my arm as I shuffled out to the van.

Mary said, "Open your planner and write down what you bought. Do you remember what you bought?"

I opened the book and sat there. I was confused.

"You bought a timer. Write 'timer' in you planner," she said.

Through blurred vision I scribbled in my book and knew I had done something right. My head was pounding, my stomach was in knots and I could no longer speak. The blue sky was too far away for me to see but I remembered those delicate clouds. I imagined the fluffy arms of those children reaching for the cookie tray coming out of my oven.

CHAPTER ELEVEN

Emerging

Transitions was a blessing. I diligently completed my assignments and worked so hard in the cooking class that within a short time I became the group's leader. Best of all, my confidence grew and winning games became easy!

The supervised field trips to public places exposed me repeatedly to new environments. Since I was always safely under a counselor's care, I became self-assured and looked forward to them. Over time, being out in public became less stressful. I was able to adapt to the sights and sounds. Eventually I decided to resume driving independently.

Daniel was on edge about my new goal. For an entire week, I left the house by myself to practice in a nearby parking lot. The first morning I got into the car to drive myself to rehab was nerve-racking for him. He felt that driving, especially on the highway, would be too challenging. I was determined to reclaim this important piece of freedom and nothing was going to stop me.

"You are not ready to drive," Daniel said as I took the keys off the kitchen counter.

"I am ready," I said.

"It's a long way and you haven't even driven that route with someone in the car. How will you do it on your own?"

He was clearly frightened. There was so much that could happen, little of it good.

"I have gone there over and over with Mr. Wallace," I said. "I know the way."

"But what if you get confused or you forget something?" His voice held the first note of panic. "It's too big a step."

By now, the conversation was adding to my stress level. I began to stutter.

"I, I ca-, ca-a-an do it." Now my tone was irritated.

I walked toward the door. Once I began to stutter, it was very difficult to regain normal speech. I wanted to save my energy for the car ride.

"You see?" Daniel said angrily. "You're already mixed up. How are you going to get there?"

My deteriorating speech was not going to affect my ability to drive. But continual grilling would create problems because Daniel was talking fast and asking questions. The longer that went on, the bigger the whirlwind in my head would get. If I wanted to go that day, I had to end the conversation right away. I walked out.

The car was parked outside in the driveway. It felt great to get behind the wheel. As a passenger, it was sometimes terrifying if other cars came close because I wasn't in control. Turning the key before this long trip, I was finally in charge of my destiny.

As I pulled away, Daniel stood on the front step watching with a worried expression. But I was ready to do this. I was going to drive on my own.

The neighborhood streets were quiet and I was quite comfortable cruising past the houses. As I approached the main road, though, I began to get nervous. I reminded myself to stay to the right and drive carefully. The radio was off and the windows were shut to minimize distractions. I sat for a long time waiting for the road to be completely clear before inching out.

I constantly checked the mirrors. Not trusting them to be accurate enough, I looked repeatedly over my left and right shoulders. When a car approached from behind at a high rate of speed, I panicked. *What if I get hit again?*

My stomach knotted up; my breath came in short gasps and I drove over to the side. As the other car passed, I saw children in the back seat. The woman was actually traveling quite slowly. The small image in the mirror had made her approach look much faster. I sat for awhile waiting for traffic to pass before venturing back onto the road.

At the first red light, I became agitated because the car pulling up behind me looked like it was going to hit me. I switched on my hazard lights to let the driver know I was there. I was so relieved when the vehicle moved out of my lane. As long as the flashing lights were on, no one else stopped behind me. I thought the best way to get to Transitions was to leave my emergency blinkers on so everyone would stay away.

So I did. Even with the lights creating that halo of protection, I gripped the steering wheel tightly and continued to check the rearview mirror. I made it over the railroad tracks without meeting any trains and crept by the duck pond. I was happy to stop at the light there.

The geese and ducks surrounded their chicks. The flocks rested together on the grass, many with their heads tucked under their wings. I smiled as the male swan led his family to a miniature waterfall. Just like the day with Mr. Wallace, the scene was soothing. When the light turned green, I turned off the emergency lights and completed the trip by going slowly and being aware of other cars.

When I arrived at Transitions, the security guard was standing outside. He gave me the thumbs-up signal as I parked. He must have called the counselors from the security phone before walking over to congratulate me. As we talked, Mary Sanders ran out of the building.

"I can't believe my eyes! Here you are driving on your own. This is so exciting! Let's go in and tell everyone." She hugged me.

"I am so proud of you! You have worked so hard to regain your independence. This will encourage the others so much!"

My peers were thrilled. Any progress made by one represented hope for everyone else. When one of us moved forward, in a way we all took that step together.

The day ended beautifully when I stopped at Mr. Wallace's office. The taxi administrative center was near the train station, and he was inside waiting for the train. His jacket hung beside him and his tie was loose. The sun shining through the window gave him enough light to read his newspaper comfortably.

I parked next to the Lincoln that had been my torment and my comfort for so many months. As I got out, he looked up and spotted me. His face shone with tears in the soft afternoon light. He straightened his tie and put on his jacket as he walked out.

"Well, Mrs. Sherman. I am so happy to see you." He wiped his tears with a handkerchief. "And look at you driving!"

"Mr. Wallace," I said, "I came today to show you that I'm getting better. You took care of me when I couldn't even speak, and today I can tell you how much I appreciate you, and how grateful I am for all the care you've given me."

Mr. Wallace and I embraced in the golden light, exchanging a special love only he and I could share. He had seen my fragility, like that of a flower trying to touch heaven after surviving a torrential downpour. His indescribable compassion for a total stranger had brought the sun a little closer day after day, showering me with the warmth of his heart. He was truly an angel God had stationed along my path.

On my last day at Transitions, I was blessed with one of the most touching moments of my life. The staff and other clients made me the guest of honor at a very special celebration. Not only did my friends find different butterfly gifts but as a group they presented me with a star-shaped gold keychain. Inside the card they had written *Let Your Dreams Soar.*

At home, I faced a different atmosphere. Initially I had hated Daniel for not understanding brain injury. I thought he should have joined the caregiver support group. If he'd been unable to see what was in my head before the accident then seeing it after was impossible. Even I didn't know what was going on in there. As the more mentally capable one in the marriage, I thought he should have tried harder.

Every day I felt pressure from him for the old me to return. I resented that, and I hated the noise of the TV and the radio. After months of seeing how easily I could be pushed into a mental tornado, it seemed callous for him to use sound to keep me away. The kids hollered and banged around because they were too young to control themselves. An adult didn't have that excuse.

I disliked his impatience with the kids as he struggled to cope with their needs and fears. His unwillingness to visit me during the day at Transitions also upset me. Other families brought their children to eat lunch with their parents, and I wanted to see my kids occasionally. Even though it gnawed at me, I never said anything. Daniel disliked hospitals so I pretended to let it go. But it traveled to the pit where depression lived and stuffed my secret suitcase past bursting.

Not that having a brain injury qualified me for sainthood. At times I'm sure my judgments were unduly harsh...because I was in so much pain, because I was so upset with my disabilities, because I was so desperate to hide how terrible a person I must have been to deserve such punishment.

While Daniel became irritated, I didn't have the emotional capacity to express my feelings. I had never shared the worst of my secrets, not even with anyone at Transitions, so there was no way I could open up to Daniel. If he said something upsetting,

I made my way upstairs to cry in my bedroom like the helpless child I had been under my parents' rule. I didn't believe he had the ability to truly understand how the brain injury had changed my life.

I blamed my emotional upheaval on the injury, yet the cesspool of my life had overflowed with "stinking thinking" years before. I was mad at the world and irritated by everything. I didn't know who else to hate besides Daniel…until I focused on God. He was another male figure who refused to make a showing in my time of need. I decided He had checked out an awful lot during my battles with life.

Since God had rejected me so long ago, I figured my husband would certainly reject me if I didn't get better. Disabled, I had nothing to offer. Since I didn't see many rehab clients capable of leading a highly productive life, my hopes of being happy disintegrated like dust in a grave. It was easier for me if I pushed Daniel away before he had a chance to push me. While I struggled to rebuild my most basic skills, I gave up on our marriage.

When I was released from rehab in August, what should have been a happy time threw more obstacles in my path. I had some serious adjustments to make. I had my life back as a wife and mother with needy kids and a desperate husband. Everything was intimidating and over-stimulating.

Daniel had to grasp how different life was going to be with his "new" wife and I had to accept that the disabilities were permanent. At home, though, there weren't any skilled counselors to build me up with praise and pats on the back. Any irritability Daniel showed ate away at my already fragile ego. I thought he didn't like me and withdrew even more.

He tried to offer comfort but I generally wasn't receptive. The times when I approached him, he was usually so frustrated my meager efforts weren't enough. Our attempts at intimacy never coincided and the whirlwind of life spun us further and further apart.

In December of 1996, I was working hard to regain my ability to move. Powell had relocated his physical therapy practice to a new town. He rented the space, which was a large open area, from a doctor. To my immense relief, there wasn't a single private treatment room into which we would disappear.

However, the new situation was extraordinarily taxing. The exercise equipment was so close together I not only had to weave through the room, I often had to step over support struts. The new layout was confusing and the music was very loud. After the aides put me through an intense workout, I was exhausted and over-stimulated.

Powell had planned it that way. The doctor who owned the facility was out that day. He had the only private office. Powell made some excuse to take me in there. The moment the door shut, his hands were all over me, grabbing and squeezing. He began kissing me aggressively. It was like the frat party all over again.

This time I fought back. As I struggled against his hands and mouth, he drew back with a strange look. He said, "You never fought me off when I first started treating you."

I stumbled out of the building. I put the car in gear and drove from the lot, horrified by his words. *You never fought me off before,* he'd said. He'd done that before? How many times? *How far had he gone?*

At the first intersection, a car pulled up beside me. It was Powell. I screamed at him to never do that again. He apologized. I drove home haunted by his words, by my college trauma, by my inability to defend myself from the tiniest part of everything that was crashing down on me.

CHAPTER TWELVE

Fluttering

B y this time, my recovery had progressed to the point that I was able to communicate well so long as I wasn't under stress. If I initiated a conversation, I was normally quite coherent. Only when demands were made did the word-finding issue crop up.

Even though I was finally able to get around by myself, my balance was so poor I fell continually. In December of 1996, I teetered off the single step from the kitchen into the garage. When I landed, my right ankle was badly sprained. Although I could have healed from that, the doctor put the cast on too tightly. By the time we knew something was wrong, I had a severe case of nerve damage called reflex sympathetic dystrophy (RSD).

The condition was serious. Left untreated, it could lead to amputation. It also caused pain so excruciating that I couldn't bear weight or tolerate anything touching the foot, not even a bed sheet at night. That whole winter and spring, I went back to physical therapy five days a week.

Of the different treatments to stop the progression of RSD, one of them is to have it massaged. Due to the nature of the damage, the nerves were so agitated the therapy was painful. I had to force myself to let people touch my foot. Each time, I moaned with pain.

For part of the sessions my foot was submerged in extremely cold water then in hot water. This was supposed to help the nerves get used to different stimuli and eventually calm down. It hurt so much that no amount of bracing for the pain could stop me from yelling. Many patients had similar reactions to discomfort, and everyone at the clinic was used to hearing patients groan or curse behind closed doors.

Once the RSD became an issue, there was no room to worry about whether to rebuild the relationship with Daniel. I was running a race to save the foot and I was running it alone. That bad fall led to more anger toward life, Daniel and God. Eventually all that acid poured onto my already scalded sense of self: terrible things were happening because I was worthless.

The vertigo hadn't abated much. Clearly I had balance problems when trying to walk. Sitting down or getting up was also still so challenging that assistance was necessary. My brain hadn't recovered enough even to allow me to roll over in bed. Whenever I tried, dizziness and nausea drowned me in their tidal waves.

As I struggled to progress, I also still battled with the memories. My parents' voices constantly scolded, chastised, and demeaned my every effort. I pictured myself squirreled away in that little hole behind the chair as the voices yelled; *You're just like that stupid girl. You're dumb, ugly, and a ridiculous dreamer! You'll never amount to anything!*

The old tapes played over and over. I struggled to stop them but they automatically rewound, dredging up sadness and defeat, humiliation and shame. My parents' faces were gigantic films on my internal movie screen; no bodies or limbs, just the heads and those shouting mouths, those blazing eyes.

Hatred surrounded me. There was nothing peaceful to latch on to. If I was successful at something in rehab, the short-term memory was still so weak I couldn't remember my accomplishments. The bad thoughts were like a non-stop movie marathon in my brain: the beatings, the fights with my brothers, the monsters that took over every friendly face…always the monsters were there, in my past and with the new people I met.

The only thing I could exert any control over was the memory of the frat party. That night was simply too terrifying to keep reliving. When it popped up I pushed my brain to "fast forward" through it. I never sped through the end, though. I always watched myself in the shower, pounding my fists against the cold tiles as my tears mixed with the spray. Even then my cries had been muffled deep inside.

With these unresolved issues still tormenting me, I was unusually sensitive to every compliment or insult. If people admired or respected me or my accomplishments, I felt good. If those around me were callous, I internalized it and felt humiliated. On the surface I seemed "repaired" but my insides were still in disarray.

I had a strategy in place for that, too. When my actions hadn't pleased my parents, I had given them gifts. Small ones, yes, and not something bought at the store…a trout dinner or cleaning the house usually had to suffice. But later I had given things I could buy, no matter how small. I had even given them to Roger Birk after that night in his frat house.

To deal with the trauma, to make things right, Roger needed to be given gifts. I had very little money and couldn't prepare dinner for him like I had for my father. Since I didn't have a car, there weren't many places I could go to buy him something. So the morning after the party I walked two miles to the nearest Dunkin' Donuts, bought two donuts and juice, and walked back to the campus.

My palms were sweaty as I opened the front door to the frat

house. Most of the students were sleeping late. The floor was sticky from all the spilled beer and the smell made me nauseous.

At his door I could hear music, so I knew he was awake. Knocking ever so softly, I stood there for what seemed like hours. Part of me kept saying, *Run! Run!*

The door opened. Wide-eyed, I handed Roger the bag. He looked confused.

"Thanks," he said. "How did you get to Dunkin' Donuts?"

"I walked." I looked at my feet.

"Well, you shouldn't have done that," he said uncomfortably. He fiddled with the bag for a moment. "I have a lot of studying to do so I'll see you later."

I never looked up. When he closed the door I ran outside. I stumbled into some bushes and vomited. My head hurt, my stomach hurt, my body hurt, and I hated myself.

For a short time, I followed Roger around like a beaten puppy. He paid little attention to me but that was what I had seen growing up: a mother and father living together but leading separate lives with little affection or communication. I had no model on which to build my own close relationships. I only had my childhood memories.

I appeared at Roger's doorstep with cookies or treats day after day. I assumed that because of this one encounter, we were meant to be married. I had no concept of true love yet lived in fear of him leaving me. The day he finally told me to stop looking for him, I tried to return the one thing he had given me: a scrap of toast-colored carpet left over from when he'd redecorated his room. He told me to keep it. I clung to the remnant as if it proved he hadn't entirely abandoned me.

My fear of abandonment, of being left alone, permeated all my relationships even decades later. One day while I was walking down the hallway in the physical therapy facility, I dropped my planner just outside the door to the main office. As I gathered the scattered papers, I heard the staff imitating me.

"She had to go to the ba-, ba-, ba-throoooom," one jeered.

"I, I, I fe-, fe-, feel liiike my br-, br-, br-, brain is busy," mimicked another.

"She probably has a quarter of a brain," a voice piped. Everyone laughed.

"I ca-, can-, can't lift my leg," the first continued.

"Do-, don-, don't le-, le-, leave me hear. I can-, can-, can't ge-, ge-, get up," someone else said.

I peeked through the doorway, wide-eyed and fearful. I gripped the wall and held my breath like a trapped animal. Their words cut so cruelly. Didn't they know how hard this was? To have been a star on Wall Street and a productive, loving mother, to end up having to be helped onto the toilet every time I had to urinate... didn't they know what a freefall my life had taken?

Of course they did. Every patient in their care had suffered some degree of turmoil. Yet I often overheard the staff degrade all of us. It was as if our disabilities annoyed them. They of all people knew how quickly their own worlds could plunge off the edge. Fear drove their cruelty as well as a boss who treated his patients with exactly the same contempt.

Although I had exhibited similar fear while denying the extent of my illness, none of that understanding made it into my conscious mind. The only important thing was their dissatisfaction with me. My childhood trap of trying to please nasty people was ingrained and I dealt with it the only way I knew how.

I brought them gifts. Cookies, flowers, and small individual presents were regularly packed in the bag I took to PT sessions. But the more sacrifices I delivered, the more I rewarded cruelty with presents, the more ridiculous I appeared. I was consumed with winning their respect when that was impossible.

I had been listening so intently to the insults at the door of the PT office that the arrival of other patients startled me. I jumped away from the wall and lost my balance. A woman escorting her husband caught me. As she picked up my things, the staff continued their mimicry. They were shameless and loud. I was sure other patients in the hallway could hear and that everyone knew they were talking about me.

I became the victim again. Humiliated, I clutched my things to my chest and shuffled out of the building. By the time I got to my car, I was sobbing.

For the next therapy session, I brought bigger gifts.

Before the accident, James, Samuel and I loved to go to the ocean. They learned to swim at a very young age and we enjoyed bodysurfing and building sand forts near the water. I promised that when I got better we would return. Two years after the accident, in July of 1997, I drove them to Jones Beach.

"We're here!" Samuel jumped out the minute the car stopped in the parking lot.

"Wait," I said. "Don't go running off."

"Do you need help?" James asked.

"I'll help her!" Samuel chimed.

He ran around to open my door. I still had an air cast on my right leg and getting out of the car was very difficult. Samuel was only seven but he held out his little arms and said, "Grab me, Mommy. I can hold you."

He'd seen James help many times and knew it was important that he pay close attention to my movements. His face showed how seriously he took this duty.

"Don't move when I get up," I said. "You have to stay still."

James stood nearby watching. Finally satisfied that I was all right, he went to the rear of the car to unload our things.

It was 9:00 a.m. in the middle of the week so the beach was

empty. A few cars were scattered around the parking lot and a dozen seagulls squalled as they fought over garbage. James loaded the cooler, the umbrella and my chair on top of his orange and yellow boogie board. As he dragged it across the beach, Samuel and I followed in the path left by the board. Walking in the sand was very difficult for me so Samuel held my hand.

James kept looking back. "Watch her," he said.

"I am!" Samuel was exasperated. "He's always telling me what to do."

"He's looking out for me just like you are. Thanks for your help, Samuel."

James found a spot near the lifeguards but isolated from other people. He knew I didn't like crowds and the noise of a lot of people talking. By the time Samuel and I caught up, James had set up the beach umbrella and put my chair in its shade.

It was a beautiful morning. I always came to the beach early because Samuel had fair skin and needed to avoid the strong noontime sun. We usually only stayed a couple of hours. Today I was hoping I could manage one hour.

As the tide stirred the ocean, waves crashed against the shore. At first it was deafening. I took a deep breath and mentally pushed the sound away so it became less disruptive. Exhausted from the walk, I asked Samuel to help me into the chair before he went down to the water.

He maneuvered me in front of the chair and held my elbows. I didn't have the strength in my legs to sit down gently on my own, and plopping down still made me dizzy. Once I was settled in, I inhaled deeply. The salty breeze was magnificent.

James saw me shivering and put a towel over my shoulders. "Are you all right?" he asked.

"I'm fine, James. It's good to be back here. I asked you to wait for me so long ago because I knew one day I'd be better. And here we are."

"I want to swim!" Samuel had already waded in up to his knees.

"You can swim," I told them, "but you have to stay in front of me. If you drift away, I'll wave for you to come back. I can't get up easily, so you have to stay in front of me so I don't lose sight of you."

Off they went. They crashed into the water, laughing and splashing each other just like old times. Even though I was a little nervous about not being able to respond instantly in an emergency, we were right next to the lifeguards. I could always yell for help.

As I watched the boys, I extended my right leg. I left the sneaker on that foot over the cast but kicked off the other shoe and dug my toes into the sand. On top it was warm with a moist, cool lower layer that made perfect castles. The boys kept looking up and when they had drifted too far James would yell for Samuel to move back with him.

Soon the boys charged out and dripped water all over my head. I screamed and laughed. "Guys, it's freezing!" I said.

They dried off quickly and began digging. We had buckets and cups and lots of different shovels to make a giant fortress. Within a short time it was so inviting lots of kids had joined in. I sat lazily watching them play and kept an eye on the overcast sky. As the wind gusted, dark clouds headed our way.

The lifeguards blew their whistles. "Everyone out of the water!" they yelled. "Everyone off the beach! A storm is coming!"

James ran over to help me up. "Samuel," he called, "get the towels and take Mom to the car. I'll grab the rest."

Samuel gathered up the toys, put the towels over one arm, and grabbed my hand. "Let's go," he said.

The parking lot wasn't far so we had plenty of time to make it back safely. As Samuel and I settled in, James said, "There's an old man down there who needs help."

He ran back to the beach and helped this total stranger carry his belongings to his car. When James returned he showed me a huge chocolate bar the man had given him in return.

James' maturity was incredible. All his effort allowed us to take many trips together. He not only kept an eye on me, he was also watchful of his brother. Samuel learned from James and became just as adept at helping me navigate difficult situations.

When the boys had been born, I considered each of them a gift from God. I had always wanted four children and my sons meant the world to me. By adding so much to the quality of my life after the accident, they became a different kind of blessing. Without them, I would truly have been lost.

Daniel arranged for us to go to the Bahamas. It was to be a special time, my first trip to a place I had wanted to see for a long time. It was also meant to be an opportunity to heal the fractures in our marriage.

The day before we flew out, I had another physical therapy appointment. Powell had again moved his practice, this time to a facility with private treatment rooms. My session was scheduled during the time Powell went to lunch. I would only work with his assistants.

Part of my therapy was to walk the stairway in the lobby. Since the stairway was meant for the building's traffic, it was really too wide to be used safely for rehabilitation. My arms had to stretch out fully to grab both the handrails. Whenever anyone wanted to pass by me, I had to let go of one rail or the other.

That day I was particularly unsteady because I'd already worked out on gym equipment. I was exhausted before we even got to the stairs. The assistant assigned to me that day hooked her finger through the belt loop on my shorts as I let someone pass. I simply couldn't stay upright. I pitched forward and ended my fall by smashing my head against the wall.

At that moment, Powell happened to walk back into the lobby from his lunch break. The lump on my head was already visible. The world was spinning, I was terrified to think of the setback I might just have suffered, and I couldn't see.

Powell took me into a private treatment room and shut the door. He made no effort to help or examine me. He was crazy with lust. I couldn't stop his hands and breath and mouth.

Seven hours later, an assistant followed me in her car as I drove home. Daniel had been waiting for me so we could pack for the trip. He had already called the PT office, frantic to know where I was. "She just got here," they lied to him to cover up the accident. "She arrived very late."

When I walked in the door, he was already angry. He took one look at me and became furious. The bump on my head was plain to see, I was limping badly, and I couldn't speak.

"I send you there to be healed," he said, "and this is how you come back? And the staff lied about it?"

He was incensed. He was angry with Powell for overworking me. He was angry with me for having disappeared for hours without an explanation, especially the day before our trip. When I finally told him later I was in so much pain I didn't know if I would be able to fly the next morning, his anger only increased.

The experience doomed our marriage. Either the additional injury or Powell's assault that day tripped some switch in my head. Now, instead of seeing vampires and mummies float out of or drape themselves around people, the monsters were inside my eyes. I tried looking around them but they blocked my vision. I literally couldn't see my husband any more.

We did fly out the next morning. But I jumped whenever Daniel touched me. My body thought Powell was abusing me again. I couldn't tell Daniel what had happened; if I did, he'd realize how bad a person I was and leave for good. The assault became another secret and the Bahamas trip started the death throes of my marriage.

CHAPTER THIRTEEN

The Journey Onward

The world of therapeutic touch began opening up to me. After repeatedly watching a medical massage video, I memorized the techniques and began practicing on my friends. Even though the vocabulary and protocols were unfamiliar, the work was peaceful and soothing.

It was time to take the next step. I had to fulfill the educational requirements to become a licensed therapist. Because of my limitations, I didn't know if a massage school would accept me or if I could meet the challenge. However, it was God's will that I enter this field. I had no choice but to try.

While my faith gave me inner strength, God wasn't going to do my homework. After being discharged from Transitions, I spent a year attending different massage seminars. The experience helped prepare me for the rigors of the academic world. In August of 1997, I finally felt ready.

Making my way to New York City for the admissions interview was intimidating. The first part of the trip was a forty minute ride on the Long Island Railroad. I hadn't even taken a public bus or taxi since leaving rehab, yet I stepped off the train into morning rush hour in Pennsylvania Station!

Penn Station sits at 34th Street. It is a hub for the Long Island Railroad, the subway and AMTRACK. The railroad's twenty-one tracks take up the lower level along with the subway lines. The main concourse is congested with shops and food chains. The AMTRACK station is on the second floor along with more stores. Madison Square Garden tops the entire complex above ground.

I froze against a wall while people streamed past. Signs turned blurry, sounds were amplified, and the screeching of trains along the tracks was unbearable. I put my hands over my ears, shut my eyes and tried to push all the stimulation away. But standing deaf and blind on a train platform was dangerous, so I opened my eyes.

I remained in the shadows until the last person walked up the stairs. Many signs indicated how to exit: this way to 34th; that way to Madison Square Garden; another to the ticketing counters. Long ago, the Wall Street banker I had been could have read them with a snap of her eyes. Deciphering them now meant sorting through a jumble of letters and colors that sometimes had no meaning.

I walked up to the main concourse and glued myself to the wall as more people raced by. The air cast hobbled my right foot, I needed a cane to walk, and there didn't seem to be any way to penetrate the flow without being trampled. Safety waited for me at home. It would be easy enough to slip back down to the train and give up.

Then I thought about God, about His plans for me and the way He'd been working in my life.

I pushed off the wall.

The crowd swallowed me up. People abruptly maneuvered around me, bumping and pushing. I managed to keep my balance. There were so many people closing in and flowing around me my breath stopped from fear.

I took a step. I moved the cane. I shifted my right leg.

Repeat.

I kept reminding myself of my goal. By keeping my eyes focused on the floor, some of the distractions could be eliminated.

My legs and cane kept moving. By the time I made it up to the street, I was exhausted.

The walk to the Swedish Institute was only a few blocks. When I arrived at the admissions office on 7th Avenue I was a little disoriented. The building was next to a large parking lot in a non-descript area of the fashion district. Although made of brick, the seven-story building was unimpressive.

The school took up the three top floors. The lecture rooms held fifty students and the walls sported a variety of massage posters. Anatomy and physiology classes had skeletons and plastic organs on display. Hands-on classes were held in rooms filled with massage tables. In the institute's clinic, patients came to be treated at discount prices.

Joan Marston was in charge of admissions. As I stepped into her office, I was afraid I was going to stutter. I didn't even know if disabled students were accepted.

"Hello, Debbie." She stood to shake my hand. "Please have a seat. I am so glad you made it into the city. Was the commute difficult?"

"Just a little bit," I answered slowly. "I am not us-, used to the ci-, city." My face turned red.

The small office was crammed with books and posters of Shiatsu meridians. A little skeleton in the corner distracted me.

"The program you signed up for is one of the last that allows you to leave with a diploma," Joan said. "Next year the course of study will be longer and students will leave with an Associate Degree. Were you looking for an additional degree?"

"Oh, no." I focused on her. Looking around the office was making me dizzy.

"Tell me why you want to come here. Why are you interested

in being a massage therapist?"

"I was in a car accident where I was hi-, hit by a truck and had man-, many injuries. Massage therapy helped me cope with the pa-, pain, and I want to be able to tre-, treat people. I still have learning disabilities but I have a ca-, cal-, calling."

"I am so happy you're here." She said warmly. "Your story is one of perseverance and determination. We have tutors available, and if you have particular needs, we can accommodate you."

"I need more ti-, time to take tests," I said. "Pages blur when I read and I ha-, have to read word by word, slowly."

"That's not a problem," Joan said reassuringly. "You will be a wonderful addition to our community. You'll bring firsthand knowledge of chronic pain and will teach your peers many things...not only about massaging someone with disabilities but about life. I welcome you and wish you much good luck." She rose and hugged me.

"Thank you," I said. "I want to gi-, give back. I want to help pe-, pe-, people heal."

"We'll help you get there. And I will watch with admiration."

Surely God was smiling.

I returned to Transitions to thank all my counselors for their support and faith in me. Derrick was still there but his wheelchair was gone. I gave him a pat on the back as he struggled down the hall on crutches. I told the counselors that one day I would be back as a licensed massage therapist to volunteer my services there.

They hugged and congratulated me. Dr. Benson told me I was an inspiration because I had gone so far in my recovery. My accomplishments sprang from the preparation I had received from all of them...and from the special blessings sent from heaven.

When my boys returned to school in the fall, my own schooling would start. I nervously shopped with them for supplies. As they picked out their backpacks, I selected my own. Notepads, pens and pencils, binders and highlighters filled the cart. Unwrapping and packing all the supplies into my backpack was another milestone in my long journey.

James and Samuel had watched me change, and they both felt I was taking care of them again. Every so often they would ask if I was ever going to do the things I used to do. They missed the athletic mom of the past. With serious cervical injuries I no longer played tennis or basketball, and because of balance issues running and jumping were out of the question. But I continued to ask them to wait for me.

I don't think they really knew what I meant. They were too young to fully understand it would take years for me to become comfortable with movement. When we spent a day at a local water park, James and Samuel stood at the edge of the wave pool. I could smell the chlorine and wondered what it would be like to just jump into the warm water. It was 90 degrees without a cloud in the sky.

The pool was crammed with people waiting for the waves to erupt. Every fifteen minutes a whistle blew and the water at one end rose to create a stream of waves. "Just come in with us," Samuel said. "It'll be fun."

"You haven't gone on any of the water rides," James said. "Why can't you just do this one?"

"The waves are too big for me," I said. "I might lose my balance. If I fall, I can't get up by myself."

"But we'll be right there. The waves are going to start any minute. Come on, Mom."

"Yeah, Mom," Samuel said. "You don't do anything you used to do."

"Why can't you do something just this once?"

"It's too busy." The thought of bouncing up and down and bumping into all those people without an air cast was frightening.

"It's just an excuse." Samuel became angry. "You don't want to try. It's only water. How can water hurt you? I just want to swim with you. You used to swim."

"Yeah, you don't even swim anymore," James said.

The whistle shrieked and the swimmers in the pool screamed.

"Now we won't get a good spot in the waves," Samuel shouted.

"Forget mom," James said. "Let's go."

Without looking back the boys ran into the wave pool, paddling in the fake tide as they headed toward the deep end. There were so many people I briefly lost sight of them. I panicked as I searched for their faces. Finally I saw the two of them together.

I stood on the hot concrete with sweat dripping down my face wishing I had the strength and courage to join them. They had begged me all morning to go on different rides while I limped around feeling sad at being left out. Standing at the edge of the pool, I was teary–eyed and helpless. It was impossible for them to truly understand my limitations.

Each day I thought about becoming a recluse. That way living would be effortless. Then I looked at my children. The eager spirit living somewhere inside me still dreamed of adventure.

I told the boys that one day we would take a trip to the Bahamas and swim with the dolphins. I had seen a picture of people with disabilities hugging the creatures in the warm, aqua waters. That was one fantasy I was determined to create in the real world.

Harmony filled my soul the first day of school. I walked into the Long Island Railroad station and bought a monthly ticket for

September. I treasured what that ticket represented so much it ended up in my scrapbook with a star next to it.

I even looked ready! I had on long pants that concealed my air cast, my hair was pulled back in a ponytail, my backpack was filled with supplies, and I held an anatomy coloring book so I could study on the train. I had already completed the first semester's assignments to make it easier to keep up. I was going to disguise my deficits in every way possible so as not to appear different.

I walked along the platform and stopped near a group of people. They were the experts. They knew exactly where to stand. When the train stopped, the doors would open right in front of them and they could rush in.

I stood slightly apart. I didn't wish to compete for a seat; I only wanted to be in a good position so I wouldn't have to hurry. I also didn't want to be pushed. I wasn't sure how civilized train commuters were. I was no longer using a cane but had balance problems and was protective of the weak ankle.

Surprisingly, when the train doors opened, people stepped on politely and calmly. Before entering the car, I studied where I had been standing. I found a seat and recorded a detailed description of the spot on the platform in my planner. I would know exactly where to go the next day, and every day after that.

Sometimes I spent so much time trying to blend into society I wondered how God ever knew where to find me. I wanted to be "normal." But when I arrived at Penn Station, I was easily picked out and picked upon. During rush hour, people in New York City were very impatient.

Within minutes of entering the main concourse I was knocked to the ground. Whoever pushed me never looked back. I wasn't strong enough to get up without assistance. Any of the people streaming past could step on my leg or accidentally kick my head at any moment. I was too dazed to call for help. I knew the fall would leave me with a stutter anyway, and that was unbearable.

Fortunately a police officer spotted me and immediately helped me to safety. As he asked questions, my eyes were wide and my legs quivered. *Run, run, run!* I kept thinking. The officer walked me out of Penn Station and suggested that I not travel alone.

But I was very much alone. Who did I want to be, I wondered? My disguise was insufficient. Nice clothes, schoolbooks and a train ticket didn't fool anyone, even me. In Transitions when I had stumbled, someone had always been ready to help. Here, in a major city, that kind of generosity didn't exist. By the time I made it to school I was uneasy and dejected.

I had studied very hard for over a year but was unprepared for my first Shiatsu class. The room was one of the school's largest and perched on the seventh floor. Its white walls and huge windows made it bright. Posters showing the Shiatsu meridians hung everywhere and a blackboard covered the front wall. With all this to look at and distract me, the most outstanding feature was the exit sign posted over the door.

This massage technique was done on mats on the floor. I entered the room, took one look at the mats and felt my stomach start to ache. Two years after the accident, I hadn't developed the strength or coordination to get down on the floor or stand back up independently.

My classmates were seated in a group on the mats. I grabbed a chair, moved it to the back of the room, and sat there alone. Occasionally inquisitive glances came my way. I ignored every one.

The instructor, Ted Barry, was a short fellow with a small frame and deep blue eyes. Salt-and-pepper hair capped his head and his soft, gentle voice was almost melodic. While teaching he moved on the mats as gracefully as an athlete. He always wore off-white

Japanese-style pants and jackets that flowed around him.

When he arrived, I panicked because I wasn't on the floor like the others. I rushed up with a note from my neurologist stating I must be allowed to use a massage table during the Shiatsu class. Working on the floor with a cast, balance issues and muscle weakness presented obvious risks.

Ted radiated an energy as warm as the sun. The first thing he did after reading the note was to gently hug me. He then walked to the back of the room and moved my chair so that I was next to the group. As I sat down, one eye stayed glued to the exit.

The teacher asked us to introduce ourselves and started with me. The nineteen other students looked so healthy. They had been stretching and conversing easily while I, the former banker, sat frozen to keep the throbbing headache and nausea from growing worse. In a voice barely above a whisper I managed to say my name. And then:

"I am different."

I briefly explained that I had been in a rehab facility for seven months due to a traumatic brain injury and that some disabilities were permanent. All eyes focused on me. Perhaps they were wondering why I was there or how I was going to keep up with the physical demands of the classes. Maybe they felt a little discomfort because they would have to work on me in the hands-on portions. Maybe they looked at me with love and compassion; I don't know.

My vision blurred, they became a blended mass of bodies and, after presenting my story, I withdrew emotionally. Others shared their own reasons for being in the program. I didn't hear their words because I was concentrating on ways to get up and quietly run away.

After introductions it was time for a break. I followed everyone out to the lounge. This small room held half a dozen tables and some chairs. A soda and snack machine sat to the right while a small sofa, pay phone and a bulletin board were on the left. The back of the room was lined with long tables used by study groups.

I found an empty table and sat by myself. I put my hands together and asked God to help me. I was only safe with disabled people. That was the world I knew and where I wanted to return.

As I prayed, a woman from my class sat across from me. Jane Rivilo was nearly six feet tall with light brown hair and brown eyes. Her large frame was topped by a small, finely featured face. That day she wore jeans with a heavy belt and tank-top, which I would soon realize was her everyday look.

When she spoke her words were chosen with care. She was like a still lake with unknown depths. The moment she sat down, I felt a profound compassion radiating from her. Without us exchanging a word I knew she could feel my fear. I could trust her.

She smiled, offered me part of her snack, and welcomed me into her life. She said she was honored to have me in the class and felt I would be an inspiration to her. I wasn't sure why I would be important to her but at that moment I knew everything would work out.

My wings were growing stronger.

CHAPTER FOURTEEN

True Gifts

There are people in this world who offer up their special gifts without expecting anything in return. I had nothing to exchange, yet when I returned to class after the break the teacher's assistant held out his hands and asked if I wished to be helped onto the mats.

Gary Williams was tall with short black hair, a thin moustache, dark skin and glasses. He had a way of doing things so unobtrusively that he blended into the surroundings, yet he carried a hidden strength. His demeanor was humble and his face was filled with sympathy.

When he appeared at my side in the first Shiatsu class he was like a stealth bomber. My internal radar sensed a protector; the sheer power of his spirit could drop bombs on the enemy if need be. Although he could have intimidated me with a quick flip of his wing he moved slowly, talked quietly, and later told me I had looked like a deer in headlights while staring at the exit sign.

Gary nicknamed me his angel. He believed God had great plans for me and that he was there to nurture me through the program and to guide me on my journey. His capacity for unconditional, non-judgmental love poured out from the moment he came into my life. Frequently he invited me home to get to know his mother and grandmother. Those women became the mother and grandmother of my dreams.

I trusted Gary so much that I eventually began to share my secrets with him and his mom. He taught me to hold my head up high. His home provided the first place in my life where I no longer constantly had to tread water. I could rest, even if only for an afternoon, with both feet on solid ground.

I allowed him to hold me while I sank to the floor. He sat on one side of me and a woman from the class sat on the other side. She was about average height with short brown hair and hazel eyes. She introduced herself as Patty Singer while hugging me.

Coming from the Bronx, Patty was my polar opposite yet became my closest female friend at the institute. I showed up in khaki pants and polo shirts with that squeaky clean "Ivory girl" look; she came in denim overalls, a flannel shirt, assorted tattoos, and sometimes an entirely different hair color. She had worked as a letter carrier for ten years and could keep up with any guy in terms of "shop talk;" I spoke about church picnics and choir practice.

There were no subtleties with her, which I found refreshing. She spoke her mind as if she had a little pit bull inside waiting to nip the ankles of anyone who crossed her. She was tough in a no-nonsense way if she had to be but her heart was as big as the moon. Since she had previous experience working with the handicapped, my assortment of disabilities didn't faze her.

She had a special way of minimizing anything I felt bad about to the point that I often forgot I was different. That was one of her greatest gifts. She was my strength when I was weak. In hands-on classes, she touched me so carefully and helped me move with such ease I felt graceful and safe. I admired her self-confidence and pride, and dreamed that one day I would be more like her.

Gary and Patty were instantly my companions. God's love shone through them. The class began with stretches, and they helped position my legs and arms so I could participate. Having been in a hunched posture because of the muscle spasms, I had to persuade my body to open up in an unfamiliar place.

I was also apprehensive because my right foot needed protection. The RSD still flared into excruciating pain when it was bumped. To be resting on a mat with my legs extended among so many other people who knew nothing of the ailment made me nervous.

My classmates sensed my uneasiness. Working with me was going to be challenging for most of them. Students entered the school with little knowledge of complicated diseases and neurological problems, and they certainly weren't experienced with head injury. I was a pretty complex case for beginners.

Patty and Gary weren't intimidated. They only wanted to help me succeed.

Each morning when I arrived at the train station, I returned to the spot described in my planner. Because I always waited at the same place, two gentlemen took note of me. Soon we chatted together on the platform and sat together on the train.

Frank Kelly was in his early sixties and getting ready to retire. His smile was as bright as his thinning white hair. He was somewhat short with blue eyes twinkling under bushy white eyebrows. He not only looked like Santa Clause, he was as warm as the jolly old soul, too.

Joe Sullivan had a broad smile and the warmest hugs on earth. He was thin with brown eyes glowing behind glasses and brown hair that was just beginning to recede. He was outgoing and loved to talk about his adventures in Burma visiting his wife's family. He hadn't been married long but he loved their new baby boy.

He taught me how to find the right place to stand on the platform if I arrived ahead of them. Joe had to repeat the instructions over and over but eventually I could find the landmarks without checking the notes in my planner. He always boarded ahead of me to find a place where we could sit together. He reminded me to take my books out of the overhead luggage rack, and he always disembarked after me to protect me from behind. Frank, meanwhile, cleared the way ahead.

We split up then, taking different routes up from the lower level. I faced the main concourse at Penn Station alone, and the crowd continued to be a problem. Five days in a row, I was knocked down in the crush of people. My backpack trapped me with its weight, the pain in my head spiked, and there was nothing for me to grab onto so that I could lift myself up.

Every day a police officer helped me up. Every day I continued on to school.

God covered me during my commute and sent his angels to help during class. Patty was undaunted by any of my problems. When I became overwhelmed and stuttered, she soothed me. When I needed a partner for hands-on exams, she was there. When I needed notes for different classes, she copied her own.

Gary and the other instructors taught my class how to work with me through loving examples. The students adjusted to all of my needs. As they helped me roll over or get up from the floor, they held me until the vertigo subsided. They assisted me up and down the stairs and generously gave their time to tutor me.

Rather than feeling like an unwelcome burden, my classmates became a source of comfort and support. I began to believe that graduating would actually become a reality.

Things took a dangerous turn after a three-hour anatomy and physiology lecture. I left the institute immediately after the last session in order to catch my train. I was so fatigued that my vision had faded and my ability to walk was poor. The streets were very busy as I limped along trying to decipher the traffic signals.

It was impossible. If a sign flashed *Don't Walk,* the meaning didn't register. I stepped in front of cars zooming through the intersection. Tires screeched and horns blared. Only because the drivers slammed on their brakes did disaster stay at bay. I felt only numbness at that point.

Several times after other classes I experienced the same trouble. Although the danger registered on some level, I continued hobbling across busy streets. I even occasionally boarded the wrong train because I couldn't find my way.

Four weeks after starting school, I made an appointment with Dr. Haimovic to discuss my cognitive deficits. After a thorough neurological exam he recommended that I reevaluate my goals. He felt it was no longer safe for me to continue commuting. The exertion of a full day of classes on top of a round-trip commute was too much for my brain to handle. Worried about the traffic crossings, he told me to quit school.

At the train station the next day, I cried and prayed. Frank Kelly and Joe Sullivan turned out to be angels. When I told them I couldn't make it through Penn Station alone, they tried to comfort me. But I was heartbroken about having to leave school.

They offered to escort me out of Penn Station every morning. For an entire year, one or the other of them was prepared to walk with me, escort me up the escalators, and see me safely through the crowds. It was an enormous commitment, one that was a true blessing.

God had been with me the very first day I'd watched the other commuters pick their spots on the platform. The notation made in my planner had been marked by a divine hand. By making sure I showed up at the same place every morning, He had provided me with the friendship of two very special men.

Half the battle was won. When I saw my school friends, I told them what my doctor had recommended. They organized teams to escort me to the train every day after class. I was walked from the institute to the station and put on the right train starting that day!

The system was the answer to my prayer. People I had just met enabled me to stay in school. The show of love was unlike anything I had ever experienced. Surely some of that magic sparkle was showering down on me from heavenly wands.

Lying face down on the massage table during hands-on classes was not my favorite time of day. At first I dreaded those classes because I didn't think I would ever get a partner. I was "complicated." I needed a lot of assistance getting on and off the table. Even turning over was impossible without help.

By the second semester I felt more comfortable because my friends knew my limitations. They had become quite proficient in dealing with me. Unfortunately Nancy Thomas, the instructor, didn't have as much experience.

Whenever we learned a new technique, half the class got on the tables while the other half observed the massage protocol. I was on the table with Patty by my side. Because she was there, I started to relax.

"It's an easy stroke to learn," Nancy said, "and is very effective for getting into the scapula if there are adhesions."

"Don't worry, Debadukes," Patty said. "I'll learn this one and teach it to you."

I drifted away. As the recipient, I just had to lie there. I was tired and tuned out the lecture so I could doze off. When the class switched places, Nancy would review the lesson a second time so everyone who had just been the receivers could see her perform the work before trying it themselves.

A hard object dug into my back. As pain jumped into life across my shoulder, I screamed in fear. It felt like a snake had bitten me. Terror and the inability to move sent venom to my brain. I lurched forward, trying to crawl away from my attacker.

"He-, he-, he-, help me, Pa-, Pa-, Patty," I moaned as I hyperventilated.

"What are you doing?" Patty yelled at the instructor. "You can't touch her like that! She needs to be talked to before you start any kind of work, especially deep friction!"

Patty's voice cut through the whirlwind in my brain. "Stay where you are, Debbie. I'm right here. No one is going to hurt you."

"I'm here, too," a man's voice said quietly. "It's Jack. I'm going to put my hand on your back so you know you're safe."

I was only able to process the tiniest bit of what he said. Patty knew that.

"Don't touch her," she said. "She can't really hear you right now. It's me, Debbie, and only me. I'm going to touch your lower back, Debbie. It's Patty, and I am going to touch your lower back."

I felt her hand through the towel. "It's OK," she said softly. "I'm here. It's OK. You're safe."

In the background, my classmates scolded Nancy for jamming her fist into my shoulder.

"You're the teacher," Jack said angrily, "and you made a big mistake. You'd better get guidance from someone if you want to teach this class because you hurt our friend."

"I am so sorry," Nancy said. "What can we do for her now?"

"You can't do anything," Patty said. "You need to let us take care of her. We need Gary."

"Class will resume in half an hour," Nancy said. "Let me find Gary."

By then many of my classmates had already left to find him. Patty stayed with me, calmed me down, and eventually got me to sit up. The dizziness was so severe I couldn't walk but I was afraid to stay in the room. I didn't want to see Nancy again. I leaned off the table to escape.

"Where do you think you're going without your drawers?" Patty asked. "Sit there until you can get dressed. Then I'll walk you out. No one is going to bother you here, so what's your hurry?"

By now my shoulder was in a severe spasm that radiated down my arm. My head throbbed. I was choking back tears and gasping for air.

"You look life a fish out of water," Patty said as she rubbed my back. "Breathe nice and slow. We'll go down to the lounge and take a break together."

I always listened to Patty. She knew when to take charge and she led me to safety. In the lounge, Gary and my other classmates formed a protective privacy wall around me until I could collect my thoughts enough to say thank you.

From that day on I was watched over and sheltered by one of the tightest-knit classes the school had ever seen. I had struggled out of the sticky gray sap of depression and abuse to land in a soft cocoon of love.

Eventually my disabilities didn't control me. I began to have power over my body. I stretched in class, worked on becoming more flexible, and practiced constantly on my children and friends. Each night James and Samuel opened my books and quizzed me.

They memorized muscles and bones with me and studying became a game.

I even practiced massage techniques on Frank and Joe while commuting into the city. Frank loved to get on the train and fake an injury so I would massage him. He especially liked it when I treated his tennis elbow (even though he never played tennis) and ignored Joe.

For his part, Joe was thrilled to roll up his sleeves so I could practice Shiatsu meridians. If I didn't ask for a practice session, he'd sit sideways in the seat and lean his shoulders toward me. "Oh," he'd say, "I'm not looking for a massage."

They both teased me and pretended they were doing me a favor. Actually I had to make sure the massages were distributed evenly so they felt like I was treating them fairly! Passengers with their own long commutes watched in envy.

If I had a test that day, Frank and Joe read their books and newspapers so I could study. They were my constant morning companions, always full of encouraging words. All this attention from friends, family and the faculty enabled me to develop so much confidence that for the Shiatsu final exam, I closed up the table and worked on the mats with ease.

With each passing day, I became more determined to dance in the breeze of my new life.

CHAPTER FIFTEEN

Shot Down

C eleste and I leaned against a fence rail at the Red Barn. It had rained the night before and we had walked up to the riding ring to make sure it wasn't too muddy. Otherwise the horses would slip and slop around, never a good situation for me. As we turned to go back to the barn, one of the trainers rode past.

"Who's riding?" Celeste asked as she turned her head to follow the sound.

"It's Caroline on a pretty black horse," I answered. "His coat is so shiny he looks like Black Beauty. You remember that story, don't you?"

"Yes."

"Caroline is jumping right in front of us. You'll feel her go by. She is following a set course so she'll start with the white gate, go over the brick wall, and finish with the hay bales. She's wearing tan britches, black boots and a black shirt to match the horse. She is signaling that the ground is dry enough and the ring conditions are safe, so let's go ride."

I enjoyed painting pictures of the things Celeste couldn't see. Sometimes, though, Celeste knew more about the world than I did. One beautiful Saturday morning in July, I got out of bed at 5:00 a.m. to go over my anatomy and physiology flashcards. As the sun rose and the birds started to sing, I had the urge to escape to the barn. I took my cards along so I could go over them at the gas station, in the checkout line as I bought carrots, and at every red light along the way. When I arrived, Celeste was relaxing by the ring.

"Hi, Celeste. It's me." I spoke loudly so she would recognize my voice. "I'll give you a lesson today if you want."

"Thanks. I'd love that."

As we walked toward the barn, I was reviewing the notes. "Watch out," Celeste said, "you're going to crash!"

I hit the fence next to the barn and started to fall. Celeste caught me and held me until I was stable. She had every nook and cranny of the horse farm memorized and had known by my position that I was too close to a railing.

"What are you reading, anyway?" she asked.

"My notes for the Swedish Massage Institute. I take them everywhere."

"Well, maybe you should put them away. You're lucky I saved you—all four feet ten of me."

"Yup, you're a tough one," I said playfully, "but if I had gone down, you would've gone down with me."

"Oh, no, I wouldn't. I can protect myself."

"So you think your tiny four foot figure can protect you against my mighty five-nine frame? Let's see, tough guy!"

I ran circles around her tapping her all over until we both laughed so hard my flashcards went flying.

"Why don't you sign up for that show for disabled riders?" Celeste asked.

"I can't be in a horse show while I'm in school. My brain will be fried."

"You can do it, and you should."

"I can't."

"You can." She turned toward me. "Look, I went into shows while studying for the Bar Exam. This show is low-key, and you can ride Buttons. He loves shows. I'll help you prepare. I promise it will be fun."

I wondered how a blind woman was going to get me ready for a show. Still, I couldn't argue with her.

Celeste realized that my silence meant I was weakening. As supervising prosecutor in the district attorney's office, it was her job to pick up on conversational clues. She was also well trained in persuasion.

"You see, you can't answer because you know this is a good idea. It will give you something to think about other than school. All you do in your free time is take care of the kids and study. This is something special you can do for yourself. You'll look back and always be proud." After the tiniest pause, she trumpeted, "See, I've left you speechless!"

"You know why I didn't answer you! When my brain gets a little busy I'm not the sharpest tack in the box. That's when you go right for me. I know your tricks!"

"What tricks?" she laughed.

"Watch it or I'll spin you around and tell you your ride home is in the opposite direction."

"And I'll talk really fast so you'll forget you were going to spin me around!"

We loved to play with each other in a way no one else could. We filled in for each other's inabilities. It was a comfortable match. We were like a pair old shoes; we traveled the same path together and if one got stuck, the other took the load until balance was restored.

Celeste didn't give up until she'd talked me into signing up for the horse show. She helped me prepare for weeks, especially as I got nervous the day before. I told her that it felt like my boots were sinking into the mud so fast I couldn't move. Celeste said she was going forward for the two of us. She promised to lift up my feet and set them atop her own; and she did.

On the morning of the horse show my equipment was organized. The night before a long list taped to the refrigerator reminded me of everything I was supposed to pack: show saddle pad, boots, boot hooks, jacket, show helmet, fly spray, bridle, gloves, water, snacks, carrots, horse treats, grooming box, and boot polish...for starters!

The show took place at a farm on the eastern portion of Long Island. The owners offered the facility free of charge for the occasion. There was an indoor ring for the walk-trot classes and an outdoor dressage ring.

There were so many excited athletes around when I arrived. The stress affected my vision and I was afraid I would forget how to ride. All the competitors were smiling and had people assisting them. I became angry because my ability to concentrate was quickly slipping away.

Two of my classes were walk and trot. For the first class we went in one direction and in the next we changed directions. The third was dressage. The judge asked for simple turns and changes of gait at different spots in the ring which were labeled with letters. It was just like my early shows when I had first learned to ride.

After leasing Jack Frost when I was thirteen, my horse riding career had begun. In my continuous efforts to try to impress my parents, I entered local horse shows. The used riding outfits I bought from a tack shop didn't compare well with the elegantly dressed riders who showed up pulling huge trailers with multiple mounts. I was second-hand everything and rode Jackie to and from every show.

At my first big event back then, riders sat in folding chairs under umbrellas while their horses stood comfortably inside trailers eating hay. Their show clothes were hung nearby, the smell of boot polish filled the air, and the saddle pads were sparkling white. Mothers fussed over their daughters' long hair, pulling every strand back into hairnets so it stayed neat under the helmets. Trainers gave last minute instructions and grooms prepared the horses.

I was covered in dust from riding long miles to the show. My clothes were mismatched and ill fitting. The sleeves on my gray jacket were too short and my brown riding helmet had a tear in the velvet. My boots weren't even leather; they were tan canvas and so big I wore four pairs of socks to keep my feet from sliding around.

I didn't have a chair, groom or trainers and my mother wasn't there fixing me lunch from a cooler or combing my hair. Back then I had only my good friend Barbara to ride with. Now, after a journey of pain and hardship, a whole flock of friends fussed over me like geese with a gosling.

Good thing. When it came time to get ready for my first class, my body started to shut down. Gentle hands tied my hair back and tucked it carefully into my helmet. Someone else locked the strap under my chin while another helped me into my jacket. Speaking took too much effort so the preparations happened against a backdrop of their soothing words.

When I entered the ring, the horse became my strength. I felt so free sitting astride him. As the competition began, I took a deep breath and followed the others. The instructions were simple and we were all winners. I placed first in my class and ended up with a champion ribbon! At the end of the show the athletes gathered together to hug and cheer each other. We were all champions.

As a teenager I had proudly displayed my ribbons on the wall in my bedroom. I loved to win. However, nothing compared to the moment when I was at that show being embraced and loved by the other riders. By accepting my disabilities and adapting my lifestyle, I was able to be in a horse show once again!

On the way home I informed my friends that my next objective was to enter a horse show for able-bodied riders and to jump. I was exhausted and stuttering, yet no one questioned my conviction. To achieve that goal, I had to continue working hard. I had to figure out how to compensate better under stress so my level of functioning increased.

I could walk that road. I knew I could. But the overstuffed luggage in my head, the one where I stored all the long-ago and recent traumas away from the light, was about to have one more secret shoved inside. That final trauma would make my burden too heavy to carry any further.

In August of 1998, I totally surrendered my soul. I had been living like an amoeba with no muscles or backbone. I was pliable and defenseless, a single-celled organism focused only on healing. Any ripple could drastically change the direction of my flow, leaving me to drift with no landmarks to guide me.

As usual, I allowed myself to be undressed by the physical therapy aides, draped with a gown and placed face-down on an examination table. My treatment that day would begin with a massage to loosen the stiff muscles and ligaments, and to ease some of the pain therapy inevitably caused. Alone in a treatment room with Ed Powell, I would experience total defeat.

I don't know what went through his mind as he walked in that day. Music was playing in the background much louder than usual. It was Enya; I'll never forget the songs. The constant loud sound created more mental imbalance for me, and Powell knew that.

I thought of the snow globe he had used during our first session to simulate the conditions inside my head. He knew my brain had become like a jumble of flakes and he knew how to stir them up with a quick shake. The blizzard inside the snow globe was nothing compared to the storm that was coming.

Lying face down, I let my ears tell me what was going on. He dragged something heavy and made of metal across the floor; I could hear that he moved it toward the door. The scraping sound was bad but when it stopped I became nervous. A barricade was in place. No one would be able to enter until Powell decided to let them in.

He dimmed the lights. My heart beat more quickly and I began to sweat. With my face resting in the cushioned cradle, I couldn't move my head at all. My fists were clenched at my sides but I was still so weak I wasn't able to push myself up. Even if I had been strong enough, the vertigo would have pitched me off the table.

I heard him unzip his pants. He lifted my hips so they were off the table. I was like a wounded dog down on its front legs. At first I didn't know why he wanted me in that position. It hurt my neck and back horribly and I wanted to scream. I wanted to run, I wanted to cry.

"Easy," he said. He slipped my underwear down and then he sodomized me.

The pain was excruciating. He grabbed me tightly so I wouldn't move.

Darkness took over.

The touch of the aides brought me back to my body. Powell was gone; he had left me face-down with my underwear back in place and my body covered by the gown. Although the hands helping me off the table stung me with fear, my heart was dead and I couldn't speak.

The sexual abuse was beyond my comprehension. As I drove

home the pain was almost debilitating. I couldn't cope with all the thoughts racing through my head and the emotions tearing at my chest. I kept trying to figure out why I was so bad. Why did Powell hate me?

Daniel was so locked out of my world and I was so skilled at dissociating, my own husband never had a chance to step in and help me. I had stayed hidden inside the cocoon for so long even a trauma as horrifying as this went undetected.

Like a stunned child I went home to my bedroom. Alone, I dealt with the pain. I thought of my father and the college "boyfriend" who I had trusted blindly.

The scene from the movie *Deliverance,* where an obese man is sodomized and forced to squeal like a pig, played over and over in my mind. I became an animal worthy only of living in garbage. I felt like I had been in a dumpster all my life. Ed Powell just closed the lid leaving me to suffocate in the stench of my own existence.

The agony of living simply couldn't be born. My focus turned from fighting for a better life to an easy surrender, to death. The demons, familiar and gleaming wickedly, beckoned me to hell.

I returned to physical therapy for my next scheduled session. I took a tray of homemade cookies neatly wrapped with a bow. I didn't know how to make Powell treat me well other than to present him with gifts. That was what I had done all my life, only now the stakes were higher. Earning his respect meant the difference between life and death.

Before going inside, I stood next to the dumpster in the parking lot. I was ashamed, fearful and depressed. As I looked at all the trash, I knew the cookies would never be a substantial enough gift.

"How do you make people think you aren't garbage?" I asked. "How much do you have to give them? Do you give up everything, including your spirit?"

I took the cookies to the front desk. Without looking up, I pushed them at the receptionist. "Oh, thank you," she said. "These look delicious. Let me see if Ed is free. I'll tell him you're here."

As I stood in the waiting room, I couldn't get that ugly green dumpster out of my head. One of the aides said, "I'll take you to the gym and you can get started."

I followed obediently. As I walked down the hall, Powell's laughter came from one of the treatment rooms. His voice startled me and I briefly lost my balance. As I pushed away from the wall, I felt trapped and wanted to hide.

"Ple-, ple-, ple-. Please he-, he-, help me t-t-t-to, the ba-, ba-, bath-, room-m," I said.

The aide took my arm. The confusion grew and I forgot where the restroom was. She helped me inside, shut the door and said, "I'll be out here if you need me."

I collapsed on the toilet seat crying. The pain from the attack was still heavy in my abdomen and a nauseating headache pounded unrelentingly at my skull. After quite some time, there was a knock at the door.

"Are you ready?" the aide asked.

I wiped away the tears. "Yes," I said meekly.

She helped me up off the toilet seat and stood in the hall as I stumbled out.

Just outside the door was a small podium. Therapists could write up treatment notes there while watching patients in the gym. Powell stood behind the podium. He wore his usual white lab coat and watched me come out of the bathroom.

I panicked. My insides felt like I had dropped a hundred feet down a roller coaster and ahead of me was a turn so sharp I needed all my strength to keep from plunging head-first to the ground. Powell's image fanned out into many men. His looming form was at the center with all the monsters of my past gathered beside him. Every one of them held pails overflowing with garbage.

I lurched back into the restroom. Leaning against the door, I prevented the aide or anyone else from coming in.

"Debbie, open up," she said. "Are you sick?"

"Yes."

"Well, call me if you need me."

I smelled garbage. When I looked down, it was all over my clothes. The roller coaster slammed around the corner and swayed uncontrollably. I made it to the toilet just as I vomited. The toilet became a garbage pail and I suffocated in the filth piled up endlessly by the fiends.

More gifts, I kept thinking. *Just get more gifts and the smell will go away.* I straightened up and tried to breath. Coughing and gagging kept me from doing even that. Life was not worth living.

The aide eventually returned to take me to the gym. I stepped out of the bathroom again to find Powell in the same spot. I turned away from him and started down the hall. My arms were stretched out to balance myself on the tightrope of panic. When I rocked toward either wall, I pushed myself off and kept going. I tuned out the music, the voices and the ringing phones so I could escape.

Powell followed me. "Where are you going?" he asked.

"I wa-, wa-nt, to ki-, ki-, kill my-, my-, se-, se-lf."

"Think of your children," he called as I staggered out of the office.

His voice disappeared into nothingness. If he said anything else, the words were lost in the void of insanity. I escaped death that day by suppressing all memory of the attack.

I did hold onto one thing, though. The dumpster became my new identity. Whatever small piece of ego I had managed to maintain until then slipped away into those buckets of rot and slime.

I hit the lowest point in my life. Every time I went to physical therapy I walked past that dumpster. The fantasies also took on a new dimension. Instead of sitting in the gray room with books falling on me or being chased by demons, I sat at the bottom of the dumpster. Every man I had ever known threw garbage on me. The entire staff from the physical therapy office joined in, and the weight of the stinking, rotten mess pressed me against the cold steel.

There was only one way to escape. I gave Powell more and more gifts. Perhaps the sweetness of the cookies I struggled to make would sweeten his attitude. Perhaps he'd realize how hard it was for me to cook and he'd at least respect the effort.

One day he took a plate of homemade cookies from me and said, "You know I treat you like shit."

He continued to ignore me. Both he and his staff abandoned me. The fear stirred up by that abandonment created its own insanity. I was a pig. I deserved to be kicked into submission. I fawned at his feet for fear of being "punished" again.

"I, I, I am, g-g-g-gar-bage," I told him one day. "I, I, I be-, belong, in, the d-d-dum-, dum-, dum-, p-p-pster."

He put his head in his hands. When he looked up, somewhere behind those eyes, perhaps for the first time, stirred a tiny recognition that he had wounded me. "Don't ever say that about yourself," he said.

I did say it, many times directly to him. Each time, it bothered him. Maybe there was a brief second of thinking, *My God, what have I done?* But that might not have been possible in a man with few ethics and even less conscience.

Still, there had been a glimpse of something. Maybe that's why I kept telling him, hoping he would lift me out of the darkness. He never did. No matter what might have flashed through his mind, moments later, he always treated me rudely.

At night the Headless Horseman galloped into my room, chasing me through the dark with a glowing bucket of trash.

CHAPTER SIXTEEN

Champion

"You did it, my angel," Gary said as I walked into the lecture room on graduation day. "You successfully completed the program just like I knew you would."

When he approached me, I grabbed him and wanted to hold on forever. This was the day I had dreamed about when I was still in Transitions. Now I was standing in a room with all my friends. We embraced, cried, and talked about how happy and exhausted we were because the third semester had been so difficult.

Gary didn't stop hugging me until I finally let go. "Thank you," I said. "I couldn't have made it through this without you. You've taken care of me the whole year and I'm going to make you proud of me. I'm going to be a great massage therapist!"

"I'm already proud of you, my angel. I always have been. You are the bravest person I've ever met. I always told you the universe is not that cruel. You were not going to be put through all those tests just to fail. You are here for a greater purpose, and God put me in your life to help you on your way."

"I love you, Gary."

"I love you, too. You'll always have unconditional love from me, Mom and Grandma. We pray for you all the time and we'll always be here for you."

Gary was the first man who truly knew me and loved me for who I was. He'd brought me along as if I were his daughter. I had thrived under his care.

"Hey, is there room for me?" Patty asked as she cuddled in with us.

"There's always room for more," Gary said.

With that someone yelled, "Group hug!" My friends piled together with Gary and me at the center.

"We need some air," Patty shouted. "Stop kissing each other for a minute and breathe! I don't want anyone passing out."

Put a crowd of happy, touchy-feely people together and there's no stopping the momentum. Getting hugged by a massage therapist is a little taste of heaven. Fingertips unobtrusively circled backs and shoulders. I was thoroughly enjoying the massage merrymaking and handled the sights and sounds surprisingly well. Love filled the air.

"It's time for diplomas," Gary announced.

We quickly found seats. Without much pomp or circumstance we were called one by one to the front to receive the fruit of our efforts: a beautiful gray and blue diploma. I graduated with an A average, meeting another goal. I had proven that even with learning disabilities, I could excel and thrive.

We cheered for each other. When the last name was called, we clapped and screamed and cried and, of course, resumed our hugging marathon.

"Wait," Patty called. "Everyone take your seats for a minute. We have a special presentation. Will Debbie come up, please?"

I was surprised. When I walked up, she handed me a card and a teddy bear dressed in a white shirt. *Yippee Skippy* was written across the front along with comments from the entire class.

"You have been an incredible motivator," she said. "We want you to have something to remember how important you were to all of us. We love you. You have brought a little yippee-skippy happiness to everyone here and we appreciate everything you taught us."

My classmates stood and clapped. Then they lined up and hugged me as they walked by. Our teachers joined us for a casual party where we talked about our futures in the world of massage.

Gary walked with me to Pennsylvania Station. As I held his arm, I assumed my usual posture and stared at the ground. He gently stopped me. Holding my head in his hands, he turned my face up so I could look forward.

"Your feet know where they are going, my angel," he said. "It's time for you to let them go on their own and trust in yourself. The world is beautiful and it's waiting for you to rise up like the phoenix and come back stronger than ever."

He had a softness in his touch and his tone was so nurturing. At that moment, I believed in myself because he believed in me. I clasped his hand and walked quietly beside him as my eyes searched eagerly for the first time in years. I tuned out the busy city and absorbed my friend's energy. I began to imagine that perhaps I was like the phoenix. Perhaps my wings were strong enough to fly.

"You are a sword that has been melted down and reshaped into something stronger than the original," he said. "I will tell you again that God had not brought you this far to fail. Success is your only option."

Gary had spoken those words to me often over the past year. Maybe he thought if I heard them enough I would ultimately believe they were true. He knew my journey toward self-acceptance was an uphill battle. I was continually sabotaged by events and evil images but Gary's constant nudging gave me the edge I needed.

The frightened woman who'd entered the school wide-eyed and ready to run graduated with a new sense of self. I had made it in the "real world" because I followed my special calling and was led to the place God wanted me to be. I didn't just graduate;

that day, I was blessed with a miracle. I had the opportunity to become a productive member of society. Ahead lay the remarkable beginnings of an unbelievable new life.

How sweet victory was that afternoon as I sat on the Long Island Railroad. Eagerly looking around, I waved goodbye. In the midst of commuters and screeching trains, I snuggled a teddy bear in my arms and imagined a phoenix above me and a sword at my side. Seeing my elation and my yippee-skippy smile, Gary grinned and said, "Success."

Due to my learning disabilities, I had been allowed extra time to finish the licensing exam. The three-hour test took me almost five hours. The very next day I was scheduled to compete in a horse show as an able-bodied rider. It was August 1998, nearly three years after the accident.

I was finally taking control of my life and living to the fullest. I was tired after the exam and had initially hesitated to sign up for the horse show because I knew there wouldn't be time to rest. But Celeste said it was the perfect opportunity for me. It was small and low-key, and she was happy to share her horse, Pumpkin.

Just like I had for the disabled show, I awoke the next morning at sunrise with a list on the refrigerator and butterflies in my stomach. This time I would be jumping low fences. It was a lot more challenging than the dressage classes, and the competition would be very different. Although I loved to win as much as I had while riding Jack Frost in my younger days, I knew that participating would itself be a victory.

The show was held in Muttontown, New York, at a national preserve set aside for wildlife and recreation. The grounds were small and well-maintained. Three different rings had been set up to accommodate the different classes that ran simultaneously. Lots of the classes were geared toward less-experienced riders.

As usual, looking like everyone else was easy; acting like them was difficult. Despite all my experience navigating New York City's rush hour, I froze. I forgot things and became confused. Celeste set up folding chairs and a table then sat me down in the shade. She massaged my neck and shoulders, gave me snacks and drinks, and soothed me with her calm demeanor and constant praise.

When it was time she helped me dress, hugged me and wished me good luck. The other riders wore crisp hunt coats and spotless helmets, black boots polished to gleaming perfection, and sat on their mounts with poise and grace. The horses had been bathed and curried until their coats shone. Even the animals seemed elegant as they pranced around!

When Pumpkin began to walk, the mismatched, second-hand teenager who'd felt inferior to the wealthy riders at those long-ago shows was gone. The horse and I moved together. He responded to every press of my legs and gentle tug at the reins.

It was a hot summer day and the dust rising from the many hooves was distracting. The loudspeaker was sharp and irritating. I had to keep my distance from the other horses and act quickly when instructed to change direction or pace.

I didn't falter. When I rode out of the ring, I knew that with the help of my friends, I had already met my goal of competing with able-bodied riders. In my heart, I had won. When I receive a first-place ribbon for that class, I was amazed!

Jumping was more difficult. It required more control and a higher level of skill. The fences were lined up, Pumpkin was eager, and I was unsure. As I passed the rail to approach the first jump, Celeste shouted, "You look great!"

That was all I needed to regain my focus. Pumpkin and I raced effortlessly through the course. I received another first-place ribbon, and because the total of my overall points was the highest, I was told to move to the middle of the ring. With all the riders lined up nearby, a champion ribbon was handed to me. I had danced the dance of my dreams!

Later that day, after loving and praising me profusely, Celeste asked if I'd heard her shout. When she started laughing, I finally got it. She was unable to see me at all! She had shouted that I looked good because she knew I would hear the words and not think about her being blind.

As I laughed, I thanked God for another victory in life, for my strong will, and for the incredible supportive friends who held my hand each step of the way. My wings were still growing. Like the Monarch, I was transforming.

Early that fall, I gave thanks to God once again. I rented space and opened a massage therapy office. The practice was located in a small professional building on a quiet, tree-lined street in Garden City South. A red, white and blue sign outside read *Garden City Therapeutic Massage*, and my motto was "Providing Excellence in Care."

The corner office had enormous glass windows along two walls. Between sessions I opened the blinds and let in the sunshine. Plants and candles were scattered around, and soft music always played in the background. I was giving the gift of touch.

I had so much to offer people suffering chronic and life-threatening diseases, pain and stress. My goal was to improve the quality of their lives while treating them with respect and compassion. I never forgot that day the physical therapy "professionals" made a joke of my existence. I worked toward enlightening the general public so people with disabilities would be better understood and have a fair chance.

In December, a speaking engagement on stress management was offered to my friend at Transitions, Dr. Deborah Benson. She suggested I take her place. But I hadn't been involved in public speaking since working on Wall Street. In fact, when I was required to present a two-minute lecture for anatomy class at the Swedish Institute, I had felt faint. Surely I wasn't ready to present a talk in front of sixty strangers.

Dr. Benson told me to go for it. Although I accepted the challenge, I still had some major concerns. These were professionals who probably knew more than I did about stress management. And during that short anatomy presentation I had perspired and stuttered, been unable to make eye contact, and darted back to my seat when it was over.

On top of that, the lecture was scheduled to take place at a luncheon. Waiters would be serving food, doors would open and shut as people walked in and out, and some people in the crowd would continue talking. Every distraction meant more pressure, which meant a greater possibility I would stutter. How could I handle that problem?

Preparation and hard work had brought me this far. No matter what, I had to try. I read a variety of books, took notes, and created cards with important points and interesting details.

Stress, I wrote, *is the body's reaction to change. It is important to distinguish between debilitating stress and a healthy state of arousal. Stress becomes negative and debilitating when you perceive change as a burden and rising demands as a threat, when you see yourself as a victim of circumstances and feel increasingly powerless.*

Since I'd been through the process myself, I already knew a lot about this topic!

Once I had my notes worked up, I practiced. I talked to myself while looking in the mirror and while waiting in line at the store or bank. My notes went everywhere with me, just like my school flash cards had.

Then inspiration struck. I told my children to invite their friends over every day for the two weeks before the presentation. I stood in the living room rehearsing while they ran in and out of the house. Most of the time they were playing army, so they were loud, active and very annoying! Speaking at the luncheon would surely be easier.

I arrived at the restaurant early. I asked God to bless my words so they would honor Him and bring wisdom to the attendees. When the program began, the officers shared a little about my background. People applauded warmly as I walked to the podium.

I looked out at the audience. Waiters moved about, glasses clinked and silverware pinged against plates. The heating system was blowing and the overhead lights sent down a glare. I smiled and began by talking about what a blessing and honor it was for me to be there.

My speech continued without my having to rely on the notes. I was thorough and passionate, and emphasized the importance of sharing our love, hope and special gifts with each other. That day, I shouldered the most important task of my journey. I became God's messenger.

CHAPTER SEVENTEEN

Crash Landing

Despite my successes, the monsters still chased me. Every night was a torment of evil beings and every day was a struggle to keep them away. I was approaching a fork in the road. One branch led down a long road that offered endless days of physical and emotional battles. The other led to that final peace I had wished for so often as a child.

When I was young, I often watched the dusk turn from purple and gray to black as the Big Dipper twinkled into view. I wondered if I would become a star after I died. I wanted to be a whole constellation, the brightest in the sky. I would have wings and sit on a prancing horse with a thick mane and a flowing tail. People would be awed by the majestic sight.

One time I saw a star shoot across the sky with its tail streaming behind. In an instant the light vanished. "I get to make a wish," I whispered, "and it will come true. I wish to be loved."

The childhood wish hadn't come true. I had become so isolated and tormented by nightmares of abuse that I lost my closeness to God. I wanted Him in my life but since bad things kept happening, I thought I was constantly being punished. I didn't even feel worthy of taking care of my children.

Although I had buried the memory of Powell's aggression, the monsters came after me with a vengeance. As winter became spring the pails of garbage they threw grew ever higher, towering mounds I could never climb out of.

Every time I crossed a bridge I imagined jumping off, and when I opened my medicine cabinet I always counted the bottles of pain pills. I emptied the pills into my hand and stared at them before dumping them back into the cabinet.

In a strange way handling the pills became a ritual. They had been prescribed for physical pain but in a high enough dosage, they would cure my emotional pain. The ritual assured me there was an easy way to die when the time was right. I wasn't sure when it would come but death consumed my every waking moment.

Of all my secrets, I kept my thoughts of suicide well hidden. No one could ever know. If they did, they might help me learn to live. I deserved to die. I was confused and despondent and, despite His hand working in my life, I didn't believe God could ever love me again. I felt so weak and afraid. The place where I lived was so lowly and frightening; I was terrified no one would *want* to reach out to me.

My rehabilitation had been extensive. As a former Wall Street banker, riding instructor and the active mother of four boys, I found it incredibly difficult to accept traumatic brain injury and permanent disability. My marriage had failed, I was unable to take care of my children, I was a burden to everyone, and I had no confidence in my ability to be truly productive.

This new life of chronic pain, confusion, dependence and sexual abuse by a so-called caregiver were so horrifying that death was the only escape. One beautiful spring day while a morning dove roosted in the tree out front I drove my car into the garage, sat in the growing fumes, and begged for death.

My freefall ended. I crashed at the absolute lowest level a human could reach. There was no hope. Only God's love and compassion could help me survive. And it had to come in the form of a miracle because my time on earth was ticking through its last few minutes.

Since the accident, reliving those suppressed memories of life-long abuse had been my constant torment. Not only did I have to struggle to reestablish a place for myself in the world but my efforts were constantly thwarted by ongoing hardships and prior traumas. All that suffering eradicated any memory of God's goodness.

Plus, I didn't know how to ask for a miracle. Maybe there were specific requirements I had to meet before initiating that kind of prayer. Maybe it could only be done in church or after a long penitence. Without any notion of how God operated in the world and nothing to offer Him in exchange, I was sure He wouldn't listen.

I got out of the car and standing at the entrance of the garage, I took one last look at life. The magnificent sunset and streaks of orange and pink would have mesmerized me any other evening. Today, though, I felt no passion for the beauty. The dove flew by me but her calls fell on deaf ears.

I slammed shut the garage door, climbed into the car, checked the windows to make sure they were tightly closed and started the engine. When enough carbon monoxide filled my lungs, I would simply fall asleep. It would be painless and permanent. There were no thoughts of my children, friends or family, just a longing to end the fear.

Staying alive had become too painful. If hell was a place of fire, punishment and suffering, then I truly believed I was already burning. Living was my greatest fear because trauma was everywhere...in my dreams and fantasies, in my past and present, at home and the medical center. Safety was in death's arms.

My breathing slowed. My head drooped and I refused to move as my life strangled on the fumes. When my body weakened and surrendered, my heart opened. With a single cry I looked up and asked, "Can you love me?" And there was God!

A great surge of heat started at the top of my head and traveled through my body. The motion was gentle and soothing. It was

God's answer to my prayer. As beautiful as that reassurance was from God, it could have come at a time that was not so desperately painful.

This exact sensation had first come to me many years before. My mother had been hospitalized during her final days battling cancer. When I sat at her bedside praying, my body had tingled with heat and light had enveloped my being.

Back then I had asked that my words would soothe my mother as she approached death. Now my heart's prayer had brought the same Spirit again to help me face life. Somewhere during my journey I had lost the miracle God had sent just for me. Without it, I was dangerously alone in that garage.

I leaned forward and shut off the car.

The heat proved God was there. Even though I had forgotten the power of His compassion and had felt unworthy of existing in His creation, His unconditional love gave me the gift of a new life. He had promised my mother eternal life in heaven; for me, there was now an ounce of hope in my heart. No matter what happened, I would face life holding His hand.

With His grace I was able to climb out of the car and open the garage door. At first I shielded my eyes, afraid to return to the world that had caused me so much misery. With my first step, the splendor of life surprised me. The dove was perched in a nearby tree. With my spiritual rebirth complete she took flight, climbing toward heaven. I wondered why I had been blind to her beauty before.

As the sky darkened, brilliant stars appeared along with the faint outline of the moon. I took a deep breath of the crisp twilight air and realized how close I had come to dying. For so long I had been afraid to ask God or anyone for help.

Now I understood His purpose. I needed to "awaken" the suffering and abuse I had stuffed into that secret place deep inside. A world of trauma had been frozen inside my subconscious, crippling my ability to live fully. By facing it, I would jettison the baggage and be able to soar.

This was the beginning of a new existence. That meant saying goodbye to the old views and finding a new vision that was healthy. I needed to accept my disabilities, cling to the idea that there is always hope for something better to come, and find it in my heart to forgive the unforgivable. As terrifying as the monsters had become, they were simply fleeting, incomplete pictures of unresolved traumas.

I had been lost and helpless for such a long time. God's love made sure that this was not the end; it was just beginning. He wished for me to become stronger than I had ever been before. He wanted me to reinvent my life and create a self-portrait that was divinely inspired.

I pictured myself atop a mountain. Rainbows danced around me, the wind from eagles' wings caressed my face, clouds cloaked me with warmth, and I called the stars my friends. I had nowhere to go but up and I dreamed of sharing my world, my knowledge and my vision.

My new life as a star gazer had begun.

My family never knew about my suicide attempt. But I had to do something so I could acquire the tools I needed to face life's ups and downs. In August of 1999, months after trying to die, I found the strength to seek psychotherapy. By facing the demons and by holding God at the center of my life I could follow the light of the stars, and set my new goals.

Dr. Leslie Nadler and Dr. John Cecero, two exceptional psychologists, helped me understand why I looked at life through a dirty filter. My father's severe depression, which left him hospitalized several times, had caused his imbalance. His disease went virtually untreated. It affected his role as a parent and husband, and compromised the quality of his life.

This left my mother to raise five children as if she were a single parent while attempting to keep pressure off my father. Overburdened and working full-time, she had little energy left for nurturing. Since she had been raised by unemotional parents with unrelenting standards, the cycle was perpetuated. Not until much later in life did she find her own personal relationship with God and finally become outwardly loving.

By subjugating my needs to my parents and all the people who came later, my own mental illness had taken over. As I began to heal emotionally, a new world opened up. The more of the past I shed, the higher I flew.

Part of my healing could only happen if I faced what Ed Powell had done. When the memory of that day finally surfaced, my therapist encouraged me to let it all out. Yelling, screaming, and curses I had never used before flowed from my mouth as fury. Frustration and betrayal rumbled into their own storm.

And I didn't just do that in the safe confines of the therapist's office. I knew where Powell lived. I drove the same route to the same street to yell at the same house every week for months. The anger pot was boiling over and the blistering flood raged toward his home.

"Where are you now, you stupid bastard?" I screamed. "Why don't you start laughing at me here when I'm able to speak? You're going to pay. You brought me to hell and now I'm back! You abused a child, you son of a bitch? Now deal with an adult who can make chopped meat out of you!"

Dr. Nadler encouraged me to express my feelings this way while cautioning me to be careful. He didn't want anyone to see me and accuse me of harassment. I promised that if anyone was home, I would speed past. God must have been watching over me because each time I arrived, there were no cars in the driveway and the house was dark.

Whenever I approached his street, I gripped the steering wheel until my hands hurt. The pain helped me keep my emotions under control. There was something gratifying about slowly driving by his tiny home and using every obscenity I could think of to describe his cowardice and exploitation. I never stopped; I just inched by yelling through the car's closed windows so as not to make a scene.

"You bastard!" I yelled. "If I hadn't had a head injury you never would have been able to touch me. You never thought I'd remember what you did. But I remember! And not only can I speak, I can scream!"

In stressful situations, I achieved the best outcome if I practiced what I wanted to say over and over. The drive-bys were preparation for the day when I would see Powell again. All the shouting and cursing also allowed some of the anger to vent from the volcano in my gut.

Flashbacks of his abuse had stolen my nights and stormed my days. Ed Powell's mistreatment could have been the final act in the play of my life. It drove me to a suicide attempt that only God's hand had stayed.

Good conquers evil. God is good. And God was always with me.

CHAPTER EIGHTEEN

Float Like a Butterfly

M y sons endured many losses after the accident. In addition to losing a mother, the marriage slipped away. The divorce caused tremendous suffering for the whole family. Yet James and Samuel were about to experience their own miraculous journey.

By July of 2000, the boys were twelve and ten. They had stood patiently by me for nearly five years. As I had promised so long ago, we finally went to the Bahamas to swim with the dolphins.

Boarding a large catamaran with about twenty other guests, we traveled to a secluded cove. An enclosed ocean pen stood right next to the dock. We jumped into the brilliant blue water and waited for the gate to open. When it did, the dolphins swam freely toward us.

The boys were fascinated by the feel of their smooth bodies. After meeting the creatures as a group, each guest had a chance to swim individually with a single dolphin. We played with the one selected for us. We hugged her and she kissed us in return. I couldn't have conjured a more perfect time if I had owned one of those angel wands myself.

The trip marked an important milestone. Although I was unable to participate in every activity, I was taking care of my boys again. One day my children would fully understand the depth of the gift with which I had been blessed: the gift of healing. Swimming with the dolphins symbolized a transition through the murky whirlwind of my past into the refreshing breeze of new beginnings.

Late that summer, I drove into the parking lot of the physical therapy office and deliberately stopped next to the dumpster. Although the sun had already gone down, the sky was still bright with streaks of gray and purple clouds. After eyeing the ugly green bin, I looked across the railroad tracks at a small cemetery.

A light shower had left it veiled in a thin mist. As I surveyed the tombstones, I grew angry knowing Powell had sent me reeling so close to a premature grave. By the grace of God I was standing strong. I was not only going to climb out of that dumpster in front of Ed Powell, I was going to throw him in there piece by piece. His face, which had been one of the most hideous monsters to plague me, had crumbled to dust.

All those years I believed I was bad, it was actually those around me who were abusive and ill. Because I had been surrounded by insanity since an early age, there had been little I could do to maintain a healthy life force. That evening, everything was going to change.

I had called Powell's office anonymously and knew what time he would finish work. It was late and the only cars in the lot were mine and his. I walked over to the exit that was closest to his car. Like a tiger stalking its prey, I waited silently and motionless. My eyes focused on the stairwell and my ears picked up every sound.

Inside me a growl was becoming a roar. The sound would fling him across the tracks to his own grave. Before tossing his remains into that hole, the animal I had become salivated at the thought of tearing him to pieces. Every morsel would go into the dumpster. I wanted to drag him around to everyone he'd mistreated so he would feel the agony of humiliation.

A sharp squeak cut through the night as the door opened. I crouched in the shadows, knowing the element of surprise would give me an advantage. His footsteps slowly tapped down the metal stairs. I quivered in anticipation but waited until he hit the ground.

When I slipped out of the shadows, he jumped back…but only from shock. The minute he recognized me, he relaxed. He thought he had no reason to fear me. I was the doormat he'd taken pleasure stepping on. One swift kick was all he thought he needed to roll me back into the trash.

"What are you doing here?" His tone was flat, showing no surprise or concern.

"I would address you by your name," I growled, "but you're not Ed Collin Powell. You're Ed Coward Powell."

I stepped toward him so my face would be lit by the parking lot lamps. I wanted my prey to see the hostility in my eyes and to sense the danger. As I stared, he looked confused. He didn't quite know what to make of me.

"What's the matter?" he asked.

"This is the beginning of the end for you, you goddamned coward." The hair on my arms stood up as I leaned in.

"You are lower than a snake's belly. You have to get down on your hands and knees and beg God for forgiveness for what you did to me!" I roared. "You are a goddamned son of a bitch! You belong in that dumpster, not me, and I'm going to put you there!"

By now I had lost all control. I was insane with anger. Clearly shocked, Powell took another step back. He dared not speak.

"You must pay for what you've done and I'm the one who's going to bring you down!"

My voice echoed across the parking lot with such force birds in nearby trees took flight. Their screeching faded as they settled on the gravestones.

"That's where I almost ended up, you bastard!" I pointed at the cemetery. "I wanted to kill myself. Over and over, day and night, I saw myself covered in garbage and heard the voices of you and your staff making fun of me."

"And what did I tell you?" he asked earnestly. "To think of your children."

"You coward, my children weren't enough. I needed a psychiatrist and you never once let anyone know how ill I was. You abused me, you bastard! You abused me! You abused someone who was like a child. You are the trash beneath my feet!" I never stopped; I never let him offer an excuse.

"I pity you," I said. "When I bring you down, you'll have nothing to hold onto. You are the slime of the earth! I am going to chew you up and spit you out!"

He was dumfounded. I didn't wait for him to say a word; I just turned and walked back to my car. My head was cocked so I could hear whether he was coming after me. Had he done so, I was prepared to meet aggression with aggression.

Ed Powell was going down. He was no match for the magnificent tiger who not only lived through trauma but even survived the grip of Satan. With an illuminated soul I was going to take back life with a vengeance.

I got into my car and took a deep breath. Despite being upset and angry, I now had to drive home. I waited a few moments so I could calm down then drove to the parking lot exit.

The road was unusually busy so I waited. When I glanced in the rearview mirror, I saw Powell's car. He had pulled up behind me, perhaps to chase me as he had that day after kissing and fondling me. The hatred was still brewing and I silently dared him to try.

Suddenly an intense heat permeated my body. The sensation was familiar by now, and peace flowed all around me. I got out and walked over to Powell's car. He opened his door and got out to meet me.

"I have a message for you from God," I said calmly. "He wants you to turn your life around. Turn away from the dark side and follow Him."

I leaned over and gave him a hug. "God wants you to know that His message is one of forgiveness. Turn away from the dark side."

Leaving him standing there, I drove away. As the heat left my body, I knew God's words were also meant for me. I would have to find it in my heart to forgive Powell if I wanted to turn my own life around.

Months later I received a letter. It was a copy of a note Ed Powell had sent to the pastor of his church. The letter said he'd spent a long time searching for God and that he talked to God all the time but never knew if He was listening.

On that night, he wrote, *even though I hurt her very badly, she gave me a message from Him. She also gave me a hug from Him. There was light and peace. It was the first time in my life I talked to God.*

I, too, had talked so many times to God without knowing whether He heard. Years later I realized He had been answering me all along. I just hadn't been listening.

In 2001, I enlisted the help of a private investigator. I confronted Powell again, this time pretending I didn't remember much of what had happened. He confessed, detailing what he'd done without a trace of remorse.

As he wrapped up his dirty monolog, a loud click interrupted his words. The recorder in my pocket had run out of tape and snapped off.

I got up and walked away.

After two years of working in Garden City South, the massage practice included two other therapists sharing the same room. I purchased a larger suite in a professional condominium in Hempstead, New York, just five minutes from my home. Although my business was expanding, I was a single mom and wanted to be close to home.

The suite had five offices, a reception area and a kitchenette. Psychologists and a chiropractor rented portions of the space from me. I renovated it so the entire suite embodied a feminine elegance. The walls were a soft peach, serene paintings hung on the walls, candles glowed from every shelf and corner, and the doors were always decorated for holidays. The boys went to school right down the road and James loved to stop by to help out with clerical work and scheduling.

I continued to dream of a world where the magic of the stars and God's miracles would be easily recognized by everyone. I wanted to help other people tame the storms of their lives and dance in the wind.

With a sense of peace, I sought Christian fellowship. I sang with the contemporary folk group at church, attended retreats and spiritual workshops, and joined a Bible study in the spring of 2002.

The group gathered in Selden, New York, a town on eastern Long Island. A couple opened their home's cozy living room and made sure lots of folding chairs were on hand. After the study, all the women gathered around homemade desserts and the coffeepot to catch up on each other's lives.

Through that group I was introduced to Billy Schneider. He was a tall man in his early forties. When we first met, he wore a flannel shirt with jeans and was relaxing in a chair with his Bible. I noticed that his brown-rimmed glasses matched his hair and neatly trimmed beard.

He stood to greet me. His brown eyes were soft and glowed with a sense of tranquility. As our friendship developed, we learned about each others' lives. While I had been speeding down the highway most of my life, Billy had spent his days meandering along a country path. He lived to serve. He put me on a pedestal, treated me with the utmost respect, and assured me he would be one of the best friends I'd ever had.

I had been a single parent for quite some time and was very happy on my own. The idea of trusting another person in an intimate relationship was a bit unnerving but Billy seemed different. We continued to meet at Bible studies and spent weekends walking through parks, attending concerts at the beach and meeting at Christian coffee houses.

By fall I had seen his home. Billy lived in Medford, New York, which was further east on Long Island. He had a gray four-bedroom high-ranch with white shutters on a large piece of property. A wooden shed stood out back and firewood was neatly stacked along the side fence waiting to feed the pot-bellied stove in the living room.

He was a custom woodworker and I marveled at the beautiful furniture he created from rough planks. He was so different from the three-piece suit crowd that he was actually a little outside my comfort zone. Then one day he showed me his spare room. Much to the delight of the tomboy in me, bass fishing books, poles and tackle boxes filled the space.

I said yes to a day-long fishing trip. He arranged to pick me up at 5:00 a.m. on a crisp September morning. The day before, I went shopping for a new outfit. The light-blue cotton shirt I bought set off my eyes and the dark jeans showed off my figure. I packed a picnic lunch, styled my hair and even put on a little makeup.

When Billy arrived, he said I looked too nice to go fishing. Even though fishing was one of my favorite pastimes, he was the catch I was most interested in!

We spent the afternoon out on the lake. The dark water reflected the brilliant colors of the changing leaves. I sat at the rear of the boat just relaxing. It was a time to be still. Billy looked back and smiled each time he reeled in a bass, always offering to give me a chance to fish. He released everything he caught and talked about the beauty of God's creation.

Although I had not walked on a trail for a long time, Billy led me there. We sat in the boat until the stars appeared. Two geese ran across the water flapping their wings until they took flight. They seemed to touch the stars before gliding back around to the boat.

Looking down at the water, I saw my face surrounded by stars. The geese had brought them to me as a present from the angels. I saw a bit of heaven right there in front of me...Billy.

As the moon danced on the ripples, the kindhearted fisherman won my heart. God blessed me with a spiritual man devoted to Him. Finally, after fifty years, I was ready to face life with a partner as an emotionally healthy woman.

CHAPTER NINETEEN
Sting Like a Bee

Sometimes when I thought about the possibility of confronting Ed Powell in court after so many years, I felt a loathing so strong that I thought I was going to burst. I wanted him to feel the physical and mental anguish that had tormented me since our first meeting.

Although he had shown a little emotion the day I confronted him, it was primarily fear of how my actions could affect his future. His lack of accountability and remorse infuriated me the most. I often dreamed of putting him in prison where he would have to face himself…and other inmates. I wanted him to be consumed by fear. I wanted him to be afraid of living.

When I was finally mentally well enough to contact the district attorney, Powell was "safe" from criminal charges. Under the statute of limitations, too much time had elapsed. It was not too late to file misconduct charges with the Office of Professional Discipline (OPD). The process began and, along with it, my own preparations for one of the most difficult yet triumphant days of my life.

I started with imagery. I imagined flying with eagles and feeling the wind and soft wingtips brushing my cheeks. Soon I drifted away and wove a solitary path among the stars. As I grasped one twinkling light after another, I knew that each represented something good I had done for someone. The stars coalesced into a beautiful glistening gown. When I put it on, my thoughts settled.

I practiced this meditation over and over along with prayer. At first I did this in the quietness of my home. Later I moved to public places to challenge myself to stay calm and focused despite exterior stimulation. Often I sat on a bench in the middle of a busy mall. After a silent prayer, I escaped skyward just long enough to find that inner peace. When I returned to the chaos of shoppers, I held that stillness inside as along as possible.

I then became the personnel director who had triumphed on Wall Street. She was powerful and would have forced Ed Powell to his knees. Some of her strength still bolstered me and would help me speak in front of the panel of medical therapists and attorneys who would be his judges.

I certainly didn't want to see Powell ever again but there was no turning back. I was determined to make him accountable for what he'd done. I couldn't direct the events of the hearing but I could believe in myself.

There were many moments of fear. There was a strong chance I would stutter, mix up my words, or even freeze and become speechless. I was given a diagram of the room where the hearing would take place and arranged chairs in my house to duplicate the setup.

I walked into the pretend hearing over and over to memorize the path. There was no guarantee I would have an escort and under stress my right leg often dragged and my vision blurred. I would have to look only at my seat when I walked into the room. By repeating the steps at home, I could go in on auto-pilot and still get properly situated.

I pictured Powell sitting at the table with his attorney. I allowed myself to feel the anger and hatred that still filled my gut. Sometimes the emotions became overwhelming and flashbacks of treatment sessions blinked like a million strobe lights inside my

head. I would close my eyes, pound the chair and scream in rage…
and then I would take a deep breath, pray, and fly with the eagles
again.

"Take me to the sky, dear Lord," I would say. "Take me in
Your arms and grant me Your peace." He always did.

I met with Dr. Nadler to get ready and at first I cried in fear. I
felt too weak to go to a hearing and was terrified my brain would
shut down, leaving me staring blankly into space. Failure might
reignite the suicidal thoughts.

Then I remembered being afraid the first day at Transitions,
the fear of my classmates at the Swedish Institute, of walking
through the streets of New York City and of every aspect of life
before then. I had always kept going. I reached deep within and
found courage.

Huge amounts of time were spent working with Dr. Nadler
to prepare myself mentally for the difficult questions Powell's
defense attorney would ask. He'd attempt to minimize my head
injury and claim that I'd been functioning as a fully rational and
competent woman at the time I was being treated by him.

Although overwhelming documentation from neuropsycholo-
gists and the staff at Transitions indicated that my cognitive
abilities had been severely compromised, I was relentless in the
role-playing sessions. Dr. Nadler encouraged me to let the little
girl, who had been abused by Powell, rest in the lap of the powerful
personnel director. The adult needed to assume control and slam
the door once and for all on someone who didn't deserve to touch
another patient.

On the morning of the hearing, the personnel director got out
of bed. She tucked the little girl snuggly under the covers, gave her
a kiss and said, "See you this afternoon on eagle's wings."

Maureen Cook and Billy arrived early in the morning. Maureen was one of my closest friends. She was seventy years old with strawberry-blond hair and gentle brown eyes. She had accompanied me to every preparatory meeting at the OPD and had promised to help me get dressed. I was stuttering and a little confused when she arrived but she had laid out my clothes the day before.

I looked crisp in a navy blue pantsuit over a blue blouse and navy shoes. Billy ordered a limousine to take us to New York City so he and Maureen could give me their undivided attention. Before we left, Daniel Sherman called to wish me luck.

"You're going to do just fine," he said. "Just remember how much strength you've had until now. You can do it."

The entire ride I held Maureen and Billy's hands. They rubbed my back and hugged me constantly. Billy tenderly brushed my cheek.

"You have your faith," he said. "God will see you through. Have faith in Him."

"Bible groups all across the country are praying for you today," Maureen said. "You have the power of prayer on your side. Just focus on your power and nothing else."

"I also have all my friends," I said. "So many people called or stopped by to tell me they love me. Everything is in the hands of God. It is His will that I've made it here today. Good will conquer evil. It already has because I've taken the proper steps to expose Powell. Let God now direct the hearts of those judges."

The three of us rode together quietly after that. I let my head rest against Billy's shoulder and matched my breathing to his. The personnel director had found her own lap to nestle in. It was comforting to be vulnerable with all guards down yet so protected by a man with such Godly peace.

I clung to that serenity as the three of us walked into the reception area of the OPD. The investigator, Jane Simmons, had assisted my preparations for the hearing. She was sitting in the back corner and smiled as we arrived. As I headed over to greet her, I saw Edward Powell sitting along the wall. I had to go by him to meet Jane.

You're going down today, I thought. My jaw was relaxed as I smiled at Jane but my eyes had a strong sense of conviction Powell surely noticed. The energy of a violent storm had gathered within me and I let the gale batter him as Jane and I chatted comfortably.

"Gary Williams is waiting for you in a private room," she said.

Our group found the room. Gary jumped up and gave me a big hug.

"I'm here for you, my angel," he said. "Mom and Grandma also send their love."

"I am so thankful you're going to testify on my behalf."

"Anything for you, my angel. It's time to shut Powell down."

It was time. We held hands while Billy offered a prayer. "Lord, we ask that You be with Debbie today. Guide her thoughts and her words. We ask that You fill her with Your peace and that Your will be done. Amen."

I let go of Billy's hand. As I walked out of the room, I smiled for just a moment as I imagined the little girl sleeping soundly at home. The personnel director took a deep breath and opened the door to the court room. Nothing could stop the spirit and wrath of God.

The first question was so simple: *State your name.*

I lost my words. I sat frozen like an animal staring into headlights on a busy highway. There was no going forward and no reversing direction, just a screeching halt to life with panic, inertia, silence…the stares.

I stopped breathing. My mind was blank. My heart beat faster and faster. *I hadn't practiced stating my name.* Inside I was completely empty. My hands hung limp at my side and sweat seeped down my palms. My face flushed with embarrassment. No one was there to fill in my words. No one could help me open my mouth.

My lips pursed as I clenched my jaw. I tried desperately to remember my name. The little girl had run into the room and pushed the personnel director aside. When she faced wickedness, she collapsed.

The seconds turned into minutes. Perspiration beaded my forehead and I felt overheated and sick. The confusion in my brain finally triggered prayer: *Jesus be with me. Jesus be with me. Jesus be with me.*

And Jesus came. He led me up to my safe place, my own Milky Way. Instantly I took flight in the heavens. The personnel director scooped up the little girl and gave the child her own delicate dress of stars. Like a Monarch butterfly emerging at the end of its long struggle, the adult and child danced in the shower of God's love.

I looked directly at Powell. He sat with his head down and eyes averted. He was a totally different man. Like a panther sensing weakness in its prey, I threw him into the dumpster. I grasped God's hand. Unified, we made Powell wish he'd never tried to block my journey to wellness.

Not long afterward, I was having an especially busy afternoon. I'd been massaging all day and was preparing a presentation for Hofstra University's Women's Club on stress management. A dear friend of mine, Lisa Ferguson, who was a professor there, had arranged the talk. Lisa was dedicated to helping me complete *Wind*

Dancing and paved the way for me to present seminars.

"Once they hear a little bit of your life story," she said jokingly, "they will wipe their brows in sheer wonder and be glad they never had to walk a mile in your shoes."

"Often I wondered if I had another mile in me," I said with a smile. "But God gave me really big feet. Now I know why!"

As I worked on the seminar and reflected back on my experiences, the phone rang.

"This is Frank Conner from the New York State Office of Professional Discipline," a man's voice said. "The Board found Powell's behavior so reprehensible, his license was revoked."

"What did you say?" I was sure I had heard him correctly but I wanted to hear it again.

"Ed Powell's license has been revoked. He has a week to wrap up his business. Then he can no longer practice."

"Yeah!" I shouted. "You did it, Frank. You did it! Thank you so much. I can't tell you how much this means to me."

I stopped talking because I had started to cry. After a moment, I said, "I'm so appreciative and grateful. I can't stop crying. I need to hang up and tell Billy. Thank you again."

I immediately got down on my knees to thank God for His divine intervention. Powell deserved to be in jail but the only other recourse would have been a civil suit. My goal was to have his license removed, and that had been accomplished. I felt humbled knowing God looked favorably on someone who had lived such a troubled life as mine.

I called Billy. When he picked up the phone I screamed, "He lost his license! He lost his license!" Then I started to cry again.

"I'm so glad this is finally over for you," Billy said.

"I have been blessed so many times," I told him. "Now I can see that. I couldn't continue in the health care field if I looked the other way with Powell. Now I can move on."

I had another call to make.

"Hi, Maureen, his license was revoked!" I blurted.

"Oh, this is great news!" she shouted. "I'm coming over now to give you a hug."

Within minutes she was at my doorstep. All I could say was, "And now I can begin to heal. And now I can begin to heal."

In the softness of a cloudy July evening in 2003, Billy and I sat on a bench in front of a shrine of Mary. I had shared some of my fears when we first met but there were so many secrets Billy had yet to learn. I described the hidden suitcase I still carried inside. Since I had brought that into the relationship, it would always stand between us. It was time to unpack.

The case was so full; it took a long time even to open. As I talked, Billy knelt down by my side and he began to cry. I knelt next to him and he took my hands in his.

"My hands," I said. "Every time I take something else out, they get dirty."

His tears fell onto my palms and I said, "Your tears are God's love pouring down on me and now my hands are clean."

I humbled myself before God knowing that my life would begin; truly begin, for the first time.

The overcast sky opened up. Every star sparkling in the dark became a breathtaking beacon. Only after stepping out of the garage after my suicide attempt had I seen such a spectacular display. They really were the magic wands of angels. They encouraged us to live a life devoted to God, each other and our children.

We were engaged to be married that night.

EPILOG

Anyone who looks at me today would see a normal, healthy woman in her early fifties. But if a situation becomes too stressful or if I become over-stimulated, I don't act quite the same. Continual small disturbances can eventually become overwhelming.

I went shopping the other day in a mall during the holiday season. After an hour, I had to leave because every store was overcrowded and played music non-stop, the lights were bright, people were noisy, and the sheer number of wares, including vendors packed into every free space, caused my brain to explode. It felt like someone was shaking my head constantly and I couldn't quiet down the dizziness.

I got outside and struggled to find my car. I had been careless and hadn't focused enough when I parked to remember where it was. Ten minutes ticked by as I searched, adding to my anxiety. My right leg got heavy and my shoulders drooped down with the burden of life.

I finally found the car, shut the radio off and fled home to a comfortable living room chair. I sat quietly for half an hour to recover. Since I hadn't been in the mall recently, I had forgotten how difficult it was to navigate.

Eventually if I don't withdraw from a situation like the shopping center, I will start to shuffle on my right leg and stutter. This means

I am very careful about planning my time. I don't over-schedule anything. When an event might require more coping skills than usual, I prepare for it physically as well as mentally. I go to bed early the night before and keep my calendar clear the day after.

I function most effectively with a planner, a schedule, and very little spontaneity. My brain does not like surprises. Stimulation is surprising enough and provides plenty to deal with, so I don't place unnecessary demands on myself.

There was a time when these deficits made me afraid to leave the house. Over the years I have taken on life and now I go everywhere. I even go to Madison Square Garden with Billy to watch his favorite hockey team, the New York Rangers. At first I wore ear plugs, looked at the floor for most of the game, and held onto Billy as he led me out afterward.

Today, more than ten years after the accident, I still have earplugs and I hold onto Billy during the mad dash to leave the stadium. However, I am able to look around. I can't follow everything because the movement on the ice is so fast it makes me dizzy. I spend part of the time nibbling on snacks, text messaging friends, and talking to Harvey Kaufman, the season ticket holder next to us, who doesn't mind my chatter. Billy is happy because I'm there.

The issues for me today are pretty much the same as they were right after the accident except that I've developed coping strategies. Most of the chronic pain is gone. Migraine headaches pop up but medication takes care of those. My memory is an issue so I write everything down. Anyone who knows me will always ask, "Did you write it down?"

After all these years, I have almost forgotten what it was like to be the "other" Deborah Ellen Schneider. The woman I am today is really all I know. When I stutter, I know I need to re-group or just slow down my breathing to control the stress or anxiety. Even if I do stutter occasionally, I no longer feel ashamed or apologize.

I finally realized that the school of wind dancing does not have an entrance exam…just an open door of opportunity.

Once I had recovered and truly returned to faith, I understood that God was with me everywhere. I lost my church and struggled until I realized He had been there in so many ways: the dove in the tree when I attempted suicide, the staff at Transitions who never lost patience with me, all the dear friends who nurtured me back to health, my children as they picked up the slack and became my guides.

Most importantly, His Holy Spirit was within me. I learned how to tap into that divinity, especially the day of the hearing. I was in that room without any support system except Him. I have never been alone since.

And to my joy, my entire family has healed. This past Christmas Eve Billy and my son, Samuel, shared something important with me. They watched as I walked across the roof of Kellenberg Memorial High School, which two sons had attended, and placed the baby Jesus in the manger.

Brother Kenneth, the principal, wasn't too sure he wanted me up on that icy roof but I told him wind dancing among the stars with baby Jesus was my personal airspace in heaven. I excitedly handed out the pictures Billy had taken of my roof top adventure to Daniel Sherman, my sons and grandchildren as they joined us on Christmas day. My faith, God's Holy Spirit and the unity of my family came together in one glorious event. We don't celebrate every holiday with such fanfare but this one was special!

Our lives continue to be blessed. One day when Billy and I sat in the dining room looking out the window, we talked about the spirit of God and how it was time to finish *Wind Dancing*. A white dove appeared right outside the window and looked in at us. Billy was able to take its picture before it flew up into the sky.

Even though we have many feeders in the back yard, we never saw that white dove again. It landed only long enough to bring

God's spirit to us. We choose to humble ourselves before Him. In doing so, we learn that everything that comes to us comes through Him.

Although my struggles continue today, my work to educate the public about head injury, disabilities, chronic pain, and stress and its effects has begun. Presentations and public speaking engagements allow me to teach different communities and organizations about trauma and brain injury. I strive to inform the public about those "invisible disabled" like me, people whose disabilities aren't always immediately apparent.

My work continues in other ways, too. God blessed me with a special gift: the ability to love others with the same bond usually found between a mother and child. Anything that comes from me comes from Him. This special gift enables me to reach out tirelessly and almost endlessly. No matter where I go, His spirit is so strong that strangers walk right up and start chatting.

I use my past experiences to minister daily. I make a point of always finding the good in people, and offer compliments and praise for whatever they've accomplished. To do this, I can't be self-centered. I turn my focus outward and set a good example of Christian living. My every act teaches the most important lesson, the beauty of God's love.

If there is sickness I offer a get-well prayer, dinner and compassion. In times of anxiety I listen with my heart and peacefully offer help planning a different approach. When someone is consumed with negative emotions, I teach ways to turn those thoughts around. I help them set goals and establish a plan, even if that means just getting through one minute at a time.

In these busy modern times, so many people are bogged down, stressed out, and preoccupied. They want to talk to someone who'll listen. Not only am I available, I also reach out. Perhaps the best way to communicate God's love is to share pieces of my story then exemplify His peace in my life.

My long history of pain and suffering makes people ask, "How did you do it? What's the answer? What is the quick fix that makes you so happy today?"

There isn't any single solution or quick fix. The suggestions and answers I offer come not from me but through me. Every gift is tailor-made in heaven. Everybody wants to wind dance, you see. Through Him, I can show them how.

God and those compassionate earthly angels enabled me to conquer instantaneous disability and its consequences. Faith, diligent rehabilitation efforts and friendships have made me whole.

God released the butterfly from the glass jar. I pass that divine gift on to empower others, ignite their dreams, facilitate healing, help them find God's unconditional love, and awaken a sense of compassion and understanding in the heart of the nation.

This is my calling. This is my Wind Dance.

3463452